Praise for *Taking Sides*

Taking Sides is arriving right when we need it, a tool to infuse complex contemporary movement conversations with useful accounts of our movement histories and insightful analysis about how we practice solidarity. It brings deep thinking about recent flash points into ongoing dialogues about leadership, strategy, and infrastructure in ways that shed new light on difficult questions. *Taking Sides* is a sharp, brilliant tool for activists on the ground.

Dean Spade, author of *Normal Life: Administrative Violence, Critical Trans Politics, and the Limits of Law*

From the arresting title through thirteen brilliant essays, this reader is a gem. Alliances and the problem with ally politics, decolonization demands, a defense of riots, exposing gender violence, fighting back against police violence, and contesting white supremacy are among the timely issues presented in militant terms. The diversity of the authors gives depth to First Nations, African American, and immigrant views of the North American reality. This promises to be a handbook for every social justice activist.

Roxanne Dunbar-Ortiz, author of *An Indigenous Peoples' History of the United States*

Taking Sides hits a key nerve. It's essential for all who are serious about building movements, and fighting for collective liberation and a just world. The day we connect our grievances and put ourselves on the line for each other as accomplices is when the system(s) of domination will start to crumble. This book contributes to bringing that day closer.

Darius M., of rebellious hip-hop duo Test Their Logik

These essays not only are timely, arresting, and full of heart; they encompass the voices of the millions who have struggled within the corrupt history of the United States. *Taking Sides* shows us the choir of angels singing the song of solidarity and justice. I can think of no better time for our collective voice to be heard. This book symbolizes the first perfect notes.

RA Washington, director of Cleveland's Guide to Kulchur

Taking Sides is more than a book; it's a politic aimed at the heart of every radical struggling against a racist state. Its goal is simple: to challenge prevalent "ally politics," and replace them with an accomplice model that seeks abolition, decolonization, and strong solidarity based on equal footing. Collectively, the writings serve as essential tools for those seeking to build a new world in the shell of the old.

Luis A. Fernandez, author of *Policing Dissent and Shutting Down the Streets*

Over the past fifteen years, radicals of many colors and political stripes have resurrected the unfinished business of confronting white supremacy within and outside social movements. Their contributions have been many, and their hard work beyond question. This collection takes the conversation a step further—dispatches from a work in progress that stretches back past Harper's Ferry to the first Indian uprising on this continent. Anyone who has struggled with bridging the gap between "working for" and "working with" in their activism would be well served by these crucial contributions.

James Tracy, coauthor of *Hillbilly Nationalists, Urban Race Rebels, and Black Power*

This book gathers some of the most exciting analyses coming from today's battles against state violence in North America. Here is a movement coming of age, battling white supremacy and settler colonialism with creativity and collectivity. Organizing produces both new ideas and the reminders we need to hear: not allies but accomplices, not complacency but resistance, not reform but abolition. The authors help us rethink how we organize ourselves to meet the urgent challenges of our era. *Taking Sides* is written from and for all those engaged in struggle against a racist state, with dreams of a better freedom.

Dan Berger, author of *Captive Nation: Black Prison Organizing in the Civil Rights Era*

Taking Sides compiles essential essays for street fighters, land defenders, and anticolonial accomplices. Its words challenge the current pacifist and NGO-led narratives that seek to manage and disarm people-powered rebellions on Turtle Island, while inspiring readers to go out and fight side by side.

Franklin López, subMedia.tv

Taking Sides

Revolutionary
Solidarity
and the Poverty
of Liberalism

Taking Sides Revolutionary
Solidarity
and the Poverty
of Liberalism

Edited by
Cindy Milstein

Taking Sides:
Revolutionary Solidarity and the Poverty of Liberalism
Edited by Cindy Milstein

All essays © 2015 by their respective authors
This edition © 2015 AK Press (Edinburgh, Oakland, Baltimore)

ISBN: 978-1-84935-232-1
EBOOK ISBN: 978-1-84935-233-8
Library of Congress Control Number: 2015945903

AK Press   **AK Press UK**
674-A 23rd Street   P.O. Box 12766
Oakland, CA 94612   Edinburgh EH8 9YE
USA   Scotland
www.akpress.org   www.akuk.com
akpress@akpress.org   ak@akdin.demon.co.uk

The above addresses would be delighted to provide you with
the latest AK Press distribution catalog, which features several
thousand books, pamphlets, zines, audio and video recordings,
and gear, all published or distributed by AK Press. Alternately, visit
our Web sites to browse the catalog and find out the latest news
from the world of anarchist publishing:

www.akpress.org | www.akuk.com
revolutionbythebook.akpress.org

Printed in the USA on recycled, acid-free paper.

Cover and interior design by **LOKI, www.lokidesign.net**
Cover illustration by **Chris Robertson, www.chatperdu.ca**

All you see are demographics
All you hear is "systems"
Without undressing me down
to the sum of my parts
you cannot achieve that
checking-your-privilege erection.
You defend dogma
'cuz it's all you've got left
But
Humanity won't fit into
data bars or scripted syllabi
And won't stick around
when you can no longer see it.
Undressing us all with your politics
you become the most correct
And also an entity
you'd probably hate—
could you escape for a moment.
You steal our dignity
and undermine our friendship
When the dots connect
And I see you seeing me through
the activist gaze.
I'm not the beating heart I feel
Your eyes just reflect a
female queer blob of color.

Rakhee Devasthali

We are nothing if we walk alone;
we are everything when
we walk together in step with
other dignified feet.

Subcomandante Marcos

Contents

Prologue

Prologue

The idea for *Taking Sides* arose from polarizing screaming matches that my friends and I had with self-identified "peaceful protesters" and "white allies" during Bay Area solidarity actions for Ferguson in 2014. My patience narrowed as the long nights of exhilarating, illegal marches continued. Our disruptions were working, both as public education and political rebellion. The police and politicians were at their wit's end to control the streets, which were ours. Yet suddenly, I and other radicals were increasingly drawn into—or one could argue, distracted by—verbal battles with those inside our own ranks who, wittingly or not, seemed intent on quelling revolution, especially by policing us.

Yelling may be cathartic, but it's rarely convincing. So in hopes of both regaining my equanimity and expanding the possibilities opened by this uprising, I decided to hand out thousands of the zine-essay "Accomplices Not Allies: Abolishing the Ally Industrial Complex," by Indigenous Action Media, including hundreds in Oakland to people who were streaming out of the sort of "so-called allies" antiracism workshop that the essay condemned. Then I edited and gave away a compilation zine, *Revolutionary Solidarity: A Critical Reader for Accomplices*, which included that piece and six others. Those seven essays, in some cases dramatically rewritten, now sit side by side with another half dozen to constitute *Taking Sides: Revolutionary Solidarity and the Poverty of Liberalism*.

All these iterations have been political interventions: as provocation, as direct action to discomfort, as challenge to what I consider nonliberatory praxis. They are also an invitation to constructively debate the many thorny questions for which none of us have the answers, to hone our strategies and tactics within social struggles while tangibly looking out for each other. They serve, too, as an ethical compass, supplying directionality to walk fiercely, militantly, and collectively toward our many dreams of egalitarian social transformation.

The pieces in *Taking Sides* do not agree with each other. That isn't accidental. There are no easy or singular responses or resolutions to white supremacy, to name one brutal adversary, nor uncomplicated ones. These essays each wrestle in their own way with the dilemma of how to thwart murderous forms of social control while retaining our humanity. In doing so, they form a dialogue that models how we might intelligently converse and act in comradely concert with each other outside the pages of this book.

What the contributions in this anthology do agree on is the need to concentrate our organizing efforts squarely on questions of power. They assert that we must unearth, contest, and aim to dismantle all manifestations and structures of hierarchical power, wherever we find them, including when they appear in our movements. They pick a side: freedom versus domination, in the most expansive sense. And they see this commitment as a lived practice, inherently filled with generative tensions. The word "accomplice," used throughout this work, tries to capture this shared perspective, which could better be described as a sensibility and way to engage this minefield of a world—a way that I trust you'll embrace after reflecting on these essays.

Indeed, I edited this anthology to encourage deep reflection, which I understand to be crucial ground for serious resistance. I come back often to social philosopher Theodor W. Adorno's notion that "as long as thinking is not interrupted, it has a firm grasp upon possibility. ... Open thinking points beyond itself ... [and] is more closely related to a praxis truly involved in change than [is] a position of mere obedience." (I'm fond of adding that "an open heart points beyond itself"—an inseparable traveling companion to critical theory.) So I want you to read and contemplate the intertwining arguments laid out in *Taking Sides* with a critical eye and tender heart, and think for yourself, on your own and with others. Then carry that habit back into the streets, along with what you glean from this compilation.

These works were written by, for, and within contemporary moments of insurrection and social struggle on Turtle Island by people who I'd characterize, to borrow a term shared with me by feminist activist-writer Silvia Federici, as "street intellectuals," all immersed in anticapitalist and anticolonial politics. They all speak from the front lines.

This book is meant to have use value as both a sharp, subversive tool and generous gift. Use it as the basis for self-study, study groups, workshops, and book events, and online and especially off-line discussions. I'm hoping that you'll find it useful enough to spread the word—table with it, get it into libraries, pass it on. And while you should definitely support AK Press, an anarchist publishing house scraping by against all the odds, with your dollars, it's cool to borrow freely from this anthology as long as it's not for financial or personal gain.

As I put the finishing touches on this collection, I'm reminded that a book is never a solo project, even if my name ends up on the cover. It necessitates collaboration, and collaboration turns months of work into pure joy, making for a smarter, more nuanced creation. So many helping hands go into publishing, including those unknown ones that make the paper and ink or pack the finished books into shipping boxes. I want to acknowledge all such invisible labor, the social relations that capitalism disappears as part of its inherent logic of trying to divide us. And of course, if there's anyone I forget to acknowledge by name in what follows, know that my faux pas doesn't diminish my appreciation.

Happily, I can make visible some of my gratitude for all the care and work that went into *Taking Sides*. Thanks to those who became nearly as obsessed as me about shaping, copying, and sharing the *Revolutionary Solidarity* zine, whether in print or PDF form, especially Tegan, Finn, Doug, Harmony Chapman, Mike Avila, and the Bay Area collectives Station 40, Fireworks, and Loose Dogs. Belated appreciation to Corina Dross for the loan of her artwork for the zine's cover, and kudos to those unnamed graffiti writers whose words were used as images on the inside. Thanks also to the many folks who took it on themselves to spread the zine far and wide, not to mention Resonance, which turned the written zine into an audio version (https://resonanceaudiodistro. wordpress.com/2015/06/21/rev/).

As for the book, heartfelt thanks go out to my dear friends Finn and Harmony (again) as well as Sky Cohen, Jose Cruz, Karen Milstein, Lilian Radovac, and Clarissa Rogers for their willingness to offer mutual/emotional aid and encouragement; they all never fail to inspire me with their down-to-earth brilliance. Bravo to Kevin Lo of LOKI and artist Chris Robertson, both in Montreal, for the book's design and illustration, respectively; I couldn't have asked for better. I can't thank the AK Press collective enough for believing in this project, on relatively short notice. Zach Blue and, in particular, Charles Weigl put in untold hours of work and gave me much astute counsel, including the *Taking Sides* title along with the spot-on insight that led me to rethink and thus reframe my own essay. I also want to acknowledge those people who kindly took the time to write a blurb, and with such genuine enthusiasm.

I'm beyond grateful—more than I can adequately express—to each and every contributor whose articulate, thoughtful pieces make up this book. Besides allowing me to use their wise words,

they were all incredibly agreeable to work with, and at key points offered critiques that only made the project stronger; it was a sheer pleasure. I feel honored to walk alongside them in this anthology.

My admiration is inexhaustible for all those rebels struggling valiantly for life over death, humaneness over barbarism. *Taking Sides* is dedicated to revolution and/as love. Most keenly, though, it is dedicated to everyone who has suffered—or will suffer—the heavy pain of losing someone to systemic violence.

—Cindy Milstein, cbmilstein@yahoo.com

Brave   Motherfuckers

Brave Motherfuckers: Reflections on Past Struggles to Abolish White Supremacy

Michael Staudenmaier, author of *Truth and Revolution: A History of the Sojourner Truth Organization, 1969–1986,* wrote this piece specifically for *Taking Sides* as a historical-contextual introduction.

In August 2015, less than two weeks after Officer Darren Wilson killed Michael Brown, I drove from Chicago to Ferguson, Missouri, with my wife, Anne, and our three young children (then ages nine, seven, and not yet two). Our visit was brief: we spent about three hours late on a hot and sticky afternoon in the strip mall parking lots that lined Florissant Road, alongside several thousand other people. Like folks all over the world, we were enraged by Brown's murder, and simultaneously inspired by the militancy and persistence of the struggle in Ferguson against police brutality and white supremacy. Both before and after our short visit, we talked a fair bit about our role in Ferguson. We weren't there to fight the cops, didn't have much material aid to offer (other than the thirty-two pack of bottled water we gave away within the first ten minutes there), and weren't sticking around for the long run. Did this make us unwelcome voyeurs? Were Anne and I simply enacting our white-skin privilege, behaving like tourists in a place to which we had no previous connection, knowing we could and would leave at any time? Should we have stayed in Chicago instead?

Such questions strike me as vitally important. It is crucial that progressives and radicals constantly scrutinize our chosen strategies and tactics; if we don't learn from past mistakes, our movements necessarily stagnate or degenerate. Still, if we are to listen to the perspectives of the people Anne and I met that evening in Ferguson, then the decision to drive four hours in order to bear witness to repression and resistance, to educate ourselves and our children and people we know in Chicago and beyond, was absolutely the right move. We spent lots of time, for instance, talking with local parents who were happy to see us there with our kids. Nobody used the word "solidarity," but we stood—however briefly—side by side with real-life heroes in the fight against white supremacy and state violence.

Our brief visit reconfirmed one critical lesson from the long history of popular resistance movements in North America and elsewhere: people in struggle disagree with each other, and those disagreements can change the world.

The idea that people's collective consciousness shifts rapidly in the course of intense periods of activity can sometimes seem abstract, but in Ferguson it was on full display for anyone to see. Sharp disputes within the crowd about things like fighting the cops, the power of prayer, legality and illegality, and so on—all were quite clearly in evidence when we were there. But they played out in meaningful debates among participants in a common struggle rather than as dismissive or condescending refusals to engage with the other side. At one point, I watched a fascinating encounter between two black men in their sixties. One, dressed in a T-shirt and jeans, approached the other, sporting a clergyperson's collar, and asked if he thought prayer was the solution. The minister responded that he did, and the guy in the T-shirt then tried to convince him that he was wrong, and that if people didn't fight back, they would end up beaten down even more. "If this [the looting and street fighting] hadn't have happened," he asked, "would the world have taken notice of what was happening here?" Neither of these guys seemed like they were interested in fighting the cops themselves, but both were openly discussing the pros and cons of the tactic, in the middle of a fairly crowded parking lot where dozens of similar conversations were happening all around them.

Ferguson in August 2014 was hardly unique. Throughout history, powerful movements for social change have erupted in unanticipated places and times, and every time multiple political disputes have erupted within these movements, too. Strategic debates about reform and revolution, tactical arguments about "violence" and "nonviolence" (as well as what people mean by those words), questions of racial, gender, and class demographics and leadership dynamics in movement organizations, concerns about the connection between identity and perspective, and issues relating to the role of language and rhetoric within and across movements—all have arisen repeatedly in the history of social change struggles. At their best, these arguments have generated essential dynamism inside social movements, forcing them through theoretical or practical impasses, and then onward to important successes. At their worst, however, they have contributed to the disruption or even destruction of entire social movements. Often only a thin line separates these outcomes, and it is always difficult to know in advance when it will be crossed.

The essays collected in this book are intramovement interventions for the present moment, designed to address key issues in hopes of striking a viable balance that can enhance rather than damage our many battles. My aim here is to provide some historical context for the present incarnation of these debates. For those of us involved in continuing struggles against state violence and white supremacy, grasping the sometimes-convoluted history of current disputes can help ground our engagement in lessons learned from prior movements. In pursuit of this goal, I'll explore an illustrative—though necessarily limited—selection of historical moments from the past fifty years. Most of these examples are focused on the United States, but continental and even global connections can and should be made in this ongoing conversation.

The 1960s remain, many decades later, a ubiquitous touchstone for radicals in search of our history. This pride of place is well earned, considering that so many of today's movements and organizations can trace themselves directly or indirectly to this supposed golden era of the New Left. Nonetheless, as Canadian philosopher Steve D'Arcy has noted in "The Rise of the Post–New Left Political Vocabulary," contemporary radicals seem to speak a different language than our predecessors in the 1960s, abandoning much of the rhetoric common to the New Left—such as "the people," "alliances," and "liberation"—and replacing it with newer terms like "ally," "privilege," and "calling out." The divergence is not limited to rhetoric, though. The lessons that present-day radicals tend to infer from the movements of the 1960s are diverse, and many of them are at odds with those that movement participants themselves drew, and in some cases continue to educe.

The original Rainbow Coalition, organized in Chicago in 1968 and 1969, provides a useful case in point. The coalition was initiated by the local branch of the Black Panther Party, along with the largely Puerto Rican Young Lords Organization and the Young Patriots, made up of white Appalachian migrants.

These groups mixed militant street organizing with the sorts of community service projects that had built the Panthers' reputation from coast to coast, most famously with the free breakfast program. The coalition's demands were pragmatic, if radical: against the displacement of poor and working people under the guise of so-called urban renewal programs, and against police brutality, the ubiquitous companion of urban renewal. Both were issues that pinpointed the intersections of race and class; they disproportionately victimized people of color while also remaining persistent problems for the working-class whites with whom the Patriots worked.

The Panthers were uniformly accepted as the leading force within the Rainbow Coalition, but the coalition remained an alliance of autonomous groups that coordinated collective efforts while maintaining a commitment to separate spheres of operation, both geographic and racial. In a city as segregated as Chicago, these two types of division of labor frequently overlapped. Regardless, a shared opposition to the police managed to create unexpected examples of joint work and organic solidarity. In *Hillbilly Nationalists, Urban Race Rebels, and Black Power*, Amy Sonnie and James Tracy tell the story of a difficult early meeting in which white Appalachians resisted the initial entreaties from the Panthers' Bob Lee to join the coalition:

> The crowd of Uptown residents alternated between silence and vocal resistance to the proposal. Exhausted and knowing that the scene would be repeated on his own turf at a Panthers' meeting later that night, Lee needed to get outside and walk. Outside the church Bob Lee's instinct told him he was being followed. He realized he made a big mistake by leaving alone. Almost immediately two police officers approached

him from behind: "You know what to do," they demanded. Lee put his hands up against the wall. Soon he was inside the squad car with a sneaking feeling he wasn't going to be cited and released down at the station. Looking up he saw Patriots chairman William Fesperman ushering men, women and children out of the church. Were they hurrying home? Did they see Lee in the squad car? They did. With no hesitation, the entire community surrounded the car and began to yell at the police, demanding Lee's release. Lee was awestruck as every single person from inside the church rallied to his defense. Despite their general fear about inviting Black radicals into their community and long-held misunderstandings about the intent of Black Liberation, there was one thing poor whites in Uptown understood: The police were a common enemy. The cops let Lee go. Unplanned and spontaneous, but fully aware of the risks, the Patriots' rank and file helped un-arrest a virtual stranger. As Lee put it, "I'll never forget looking at all those brave white motherfuckers standing in the light of the police car staring in the face of death."

The coalition subsequently emerged as an important political force in Chicago, concentrating specifically on organizing youths and especially members of street gangs. Using the national structure of the Panthers, the coalition attempted to export its model to other locales, including New York and Houston, with varying levels of success.

The legacy of the Rainbow Coalition has been claimed multiple times by widely divergent forces, beginning with its invocation by Harold Washington in his candidacy for mayor of Chicago in 1983, followed nationally by Jesse Jackson's presidential campaigns of 1984 and 1988, which appropriated the name wholesale. Yet more radical forces have also taken an interest in the legacy of the original coalition. In contemporary terms, it is quite reasonable to view the coalition as an early instance of ally style politics, with the all-white Young Patriots organizing white people separately under the leadership of the Black Panthers. But this analysis misses much of what made the coalition so inspiring and effective. First, it downplays the autonomy enjoyed by all member groups. This was most clearly highlighted in the Patriots' use of the Confederate flag to symbolize their status as oppressed white southerners living in the urban North. Despite the undeniable historical connotations of slavery and white supremacy, both the Panthers and Lords supported the decision of the Patriots to use the flag. José Cha-Cha Jiménez later argued, to again quote from Sonnie and Tracy's book, that "it was really their choice to make," and "in order to really understand it you have to understand the influence of nationalism." The Patriots' declaration that white Appalachian migrants constituted an oppressed nation may seem incomprehensible today, but it was consistent with the politics of revolutionary nationalism that dominated antiracist movements during the late 1960s.

More important, an understanding of the Rainbow Coalition couched in terms of today's ally politics necessarily obscures Lee's experience as a black militant whose responsibilities (as a field marshal for the Panthers) centered precisely on organizing working-class white youths into a class-based alliance that was avowedly multiracial. The leadership role of the Panthers in the coalition resulted in an unusual twist on the standard cross-racial solidarity model in which white people use their privileges to support oppressed communities of color. Instead, as Jakobi Williams puts it in *From the Bullet to the Ballot*, "One of the most significant and underappreciated aspects of the Rainbow Coalition is the fact that 'the Black Panther Party extended a hand to suffering white folks.' As Bob Lee notes, 'that's rare in America; when white folks reach out for the help of black folks.'" This reversal is an essential part of the legacy of the original Rainbow Coalition, every bit as much as the experience of Confederate-flag-wearing white folks surrounding a cop car to defend a revolutionary black nationalist. Together, they suggest that we might better understand all the participants in the Rainbow Coalition, not just the Patriots, as accomplices not allies.

While the original Rainbow Coalition collapsed under the weight of state repression (most infamously, the Chicago Police Department's assassination of Fred Hampton and Mark Clark at the end of 1969), the politics of revolutionary nationalism continued to percolate inside the United States. By the 1970s, a generation of radicals—those who had survived the massive state repression of the black movement in particular—had either matured or devolved, depending on your perspective. As the mass tide of 1960s' popular radicalism receded into the rearview mirror, revolutionary stalwarts tended to become more doctrinaire and narrowly focused in their efforts. While many emphasized workplace organizing in factories or hospitals, and some attempted to build self-described multiracial vanguard parties like the Revolutionary Communist Party, others centered their attention on anti-imperialist and anticolonial politics, both domestically and internationally. Black, Puerto Rican, and other Third World revolutionary nationalists inside the United States founded multiple organizations, both aboveground and clandestine, in pursuit of their political goals. (The term

Brave Mother-fuckers

"Third World," normally used to group the countries now more commonly referred to as the Global South, was also used in the 1970s by many antiracist activists in the United States as a catchall phrase that included multiple oppressed racial groups, not unlike today's ubiquitous label "people of color.") These groups frequently developed alliances with each other on specific areas of work in order to amplify their efforts.

In 1978, for example, the African People's Socialist Party (APSP), one of several small black radical groups that emerged in the aftermath of Black Power, initiated a campaign in support of Dessie Woods, a young black woman from Georgia who had been convicted two years earlier of killing a white man who tried to rape her. The APSP viewed Woods as a living symbol of black resistance and organized under the slogan "Free Dessie Woods! Smash Colonial Violence!" This spotlight on internal colonialism brought the APSP into conflict with many feminists (mostly white), who saw Woods first and foremost as a victim of patriarchal violence. At the same time, it helped the APSP develop contacts with a range of radical anti-imperialist and anticolonial movements in other communities of color in the United States. Thus, when the APSP called for mass rallies on July 4, 1978, to defend Woods, it was joined by a number of Puerto Rican and Chicana/o radicals, members of the Movimiento de Liberación Nacional (MLN).

The MLN was an unusual, possibly unique, revolutionary nationalist group in that it was "binational"; that is, its membership included both Puerto Ricans and Chicana/os struggling for the liberation of their respective nations from the clutches of US colonialism. The demand for Puerto Rican independence was crucial, since by the 1970s the US-controlled island was one of the most high-profile colonies in the world. The MLN tried to use this attention to help popularize the general idea of internal colonialism, under which black, Chicana/o, and Native American communities could be seen as victims not merely of racism but also of structural disempowerment that prevented collective self-determination. Many groupings in these communities were beginning to advocate for a revolutionary restructuring of North America. This vision was indebted to the formal decolonization of Africa that seemed to be culminating in the 1970s in the independence of Angola and Mozambique as well as the developing struggles in Namibia and South Africa.

In this context, the choice of July 4 for the Woods rally in Georgia was emphatically not an attempt to draw on "American" traditions of liberty, the founding fathers, and other such traditional US narratives. José López, then one of the leaders of the MLN, was there, and later recalled in a conversation with me that "no one in Georgia that day was inspired by the legacy of the US revolutionary war as anticolonial. Holding a demonstration on July 4 called attention to the masking of a lie that was perpetuated in every American narrative, that 'we' are a democracy and 'we' spread freedom." When he spoke at the rally, López deliberately connected the imprisonment of Woods to that of others who were more conventionally understood as political prisoners. His speech was later reprinted in the MLN's theoretical journal, *De Pie y en Guerra*:

> We also come to Plains to demand not only freedom for Dessie Woods, but, also, freedom for the RNA [Republic of New Afrika] 11, freedom for the Wilmington 10, freedom for Dacajaweah, freedom for Leonard Peltier, freedom for Geronimo Pratt, freedom for Sundiata Acoli, Herman Bell, Daruba Richard Moore, freedom for Susan Saxe, the LA 5, and finally our own four Nationalist

Prisoners—Oscar Collazo, Rafael Cancel Miranda, Irvin Flores, and Lolita Lebron.

Many of the prisoners mentioned by López were themselves veterans of anticolonial struggles, whether in black, latina/o, indigenous, or white anti-imperialist contexts. While Woods herself had not been active in radical causes prior to her arrest, she had by 1978 become closely associated with the APSP, and a number of her supporters maintained that she received harsher treatment than other prisoners because of this connection to organized black radicalism.

The relationship between the APSP and MLN was notable in several ways. Both groups based their politics in problematic forms of authoritarianism, combining Marxism and revolutionary nationalism to create a coherent but limited strategic approach. Both encouraged the development of one-sided relationships with effectively uncritical support groups staffed by white anti-imperialists. The APSP, for example, asserted in the context of the Woods struggle that, as stated in a *Burning Spear* article, "the correct response from the North American community was to follow our leadership and provide our movement with political and material support." Still, when interacting with each other and other Third World groups, the APSP and MLN viewed each other as coequals in struggle. In fact, the MLN felt entitled to criticize the APSP (at least implicitly) at its own rally: López's reference to Saxe, a white lesbian, feminist political prisoner, may have been intended to demonstrate an openness to feminist as opposed to anticolonial interpretations of the Woods case.

On one level, almost certainly unintentional, the APSP helped inspire the eventual rhetorical transition from "Third

World" to "people of color" as the general category into which oppressed nations/races (excluding, of course, the long-since-disbanded Young Patriots) could be placed. It also laid the groundwork for contemporary notions of antiracist solidarity as a process of white activists taking direction from and giving support to radicals of color; this is one of the most important roots of today's ally politics. Nonetheless, whatever the problems and flaws of the APSP and MLN, both groups retained a resolutely revolutionary stance, strategizing for the overthrow of capitalism, white supremacy, and the US government. This ambition is too often lacking in today's Left, replaced by the promotion of diversity and social justice within the broader confines of the overall capitalist system. Today, many antiracists rightly criticize the class reductionism of some white radicals, arguing that questions of race, gender, and other identities must be centered in our approach to politics. Too often, however, astute criticisms of "brocialism" or simplistic "black-and-white, unite-and-fight" responses to white supremacy also come packaged with a rejection of all revolutionary aspiration. The experiences of the APSP and MLN remind us that it is possible, and indeed crucial, to pair our criticisms of oppression with a meaningful revolutionary vision and strategy.

As suggested above, many of the nationalist groups involved in campaigns like the one to free Woods appealed for support from white solidarity activists. As antagonisms emerged within national liberation movements on questions of political line and revolutionary strategy, white support groups tended to factionalize in response. Dan Berger explains in *Outlaws of America* that the Weather Underground Organization, despite (or perhaps because of) its clandestinity the most widely known white anti-imperialist group of the early 1970s, put significant effort into developing an aboveground support network called the Prairie Fire Organizing Committee. Quickly, though, Prairie Fire separated itself from the Weather in response to political criticisms made initially by black nationalists. Prairie Fire subsequently itself underwent a split, with a number of ex-members forming the May 19th Communist Organization, named after the date on which both Malcolm X and Ho Chi Minh had been born.

Led overwhelmingly by women, May 19th was a prototypical white, anti-imperialist solidarity group. As former member Mary Patten later noted in *Revolution as an Eternal Dream*, "We disapproved of 'multinational' organizations where Black, white, Latino/a, Asian, and Native peoples worked together, because we believed that these mostly white-dominated forms continued the legacies of racism and white people's assumption of leadership." Instead, May 19th chose to "take leadership" from various black (or New Afrikan) and Puerto Rican revolutionary organizations. But beyond simply opposing multiracial organization, and in spite of being entirely white themselves, May 19th members eventually came to reject the very notion that white people could possess revolutionary agency; the best possible scenario was that they might, as Patton remarked, "sacrifice *everything* to become revolutionary allies." And indeed, several members of May 19th served lengthy prison sentences for various political crimes.

Other groups engaged in anti-imperialist solidarity efforts criticized May 19th for both its dogmatic and sectarian approach to dealing with white radicals, and more significant, the hypocrisy that characterized its interaction with black, Puerto Rican, and indigenous revolutionaries. While claiming that white radicals must not challenge the leadership of Third World revolutionaries in anti-imperialist struggles, May 19th could not avoid making political decisions about which organizations, within the heavily fractured national liberation movements, it worked with. Marilyn Buck and Laura Whitehorn, two former May 19th members, acknowledged this problem in an interview from prison during the 1990s: "At times we interpreted what the leadership of any given struggle was arguing for to suit our own politics. At others, we became involved in debates inside other movements that were inappropriate for us to be active in."

Having chosen specific organizations to work with, May 19th frequently committed the inverse error: failing to voice political disagreements with the nationalist groups from which it took leadership. In a 1979 *Urgent Tasks* editorial, for instance, the Sojourner Truth Organization, an overwhelmingly white group that participated in the same anti-imperialist movements as May 19th,

> [criticized] the confusion of unconditional support for national liberation with an uncritical identification with positions taken by the national liberation leadership or elements of it. Unconditional support involves a conscious subordination of political differences for definite political reasons. The political leadership of national liberation movements must be followed on questions concerning the form and content of the movements they head, not because this leadership is always right, but because it is the social force whose correct and incorrect positions "matter." This has nothing to do with any attribution of infallibility and omniscience. We do liberation movements no favor by disguising disagreements, or, still worse, by evading questions which must be of concern to all revolutionaries.

In this case, May 19th at the very least avoided hypocrisy: by keeping silent in such debates, it simply enacted the logical conclusion of its version of white solidarity politics. The legacy of this sort of silent solidarity has been progressively emptied of the revolutionary anticapitalism of a group like May 19th, leaving little more than the politics of white guilt.

The problems that May 19th saw in multiracial organizations were all too real: most often these organizations were majority white, and either marginalized or tokenized members of color. But the alternative that May 19th put forward did not solve the problem; it merely reframed it. The act of "taking leadership" could just as easily marginalize and tokenize militants of color. May 19th certainly had the courage of its convictions, pursuing a revolutionary strategy in the face of increasing government repression. Yet in giving voice to a politics of white guilt, it damaged not only the prospects for future white anti-imperialist radicals but also the larger revolutionary nationalist movements it hoped to support.

These debates reemerged in a new way in the late 1980s, this time in the context of a resurgent anarchist movement. The discussion was pushed forward aggressively by Love and Rage (L&R), which started as a newspaper, and then developed into a loose continental network, and eventually the more tightly organized Love and Rage Revolutionary Anarchist Federation. L&R was notable for an influx of people and ideas previously not part of the mainstream of North American anarchism, including several veterans of the debates around anti-imperialism described above as well as former members of a dissident Trotskyist group, the

Revolutionary Socialist League, who had rejected Marxism and embraced anarchism over the course of the 1980s. The result, at least for a period of time, was a combustible mixture that helped generate innovative tactical and strategic approaches to social struggles around issues of reproductive freedom, antifascist and antipolice organizing, and support for the Zapatista uprising in southern Mexico, among many other areas of work.

Viewed from the twenty-first century, the most noteworthy aspect of L&R is the way in which it helped fundamentally transform the character of the anarchist movement in North America, especially in terms of discussions of the role of race in revolutionary politics. In the midst of the debate that ultimately destroyed the organization, Christopher Day reflected on this in his 1998 essay "What We Do":

> In many respects, Love and Rage has succeeded in redefining anarchism in the US—at the very least, by carving out more space for ideas that were previously very marginal within the anarchist movement. This is clearest on the question of race. Love and Rage aggressively challenged the prevailing class reductionism and liberalism in the anarchist movement on the question of race in US society and completely shifted the center of debate on questions of race to the point that people entering the anarchist movement in 1998 take for granted a whole series of things about the existence of and the nature of white supremacy in the US that were quite literally the views of only a handful of people in the anarchist movement in 1988.

Foremost among the concepts that L&R helped popularize within anarchism was the theory of white-skin privilege, which groups like the Sojourner Truth Organization and May 19th had long accepted, but that had been anathema within anarchism well into the Reagan era. Today, activists routinely utilize the general concept of "privilege" in many other contexts: male privilege, able-bodied privilege, middle-class privilege, and cisgender privilege—all have become part of the social justice lexicon of the twenty-first century. To the extent that this has been connected to the rise of ally politics, the result is, at best, a mixed bag. But in the context of the late 1980s, the relatively simple notion that white people benefited in some way from the continued existence of white supremacy—and thus needed to be actively recruited to antiracist politics and organizing—represented a necessary and powerful corrective to the general myopia of North American anarchists around issues of race (and to a lesser degree, gender). One corollary to L&R's popularization of white-skin privilege was its willingness to engage critically with revolutionary nationalism in ways that many white anarchists of previous generations had refused to do. As former member Paul Glavin observed in an *Arsenal* magazine article from spring 2000, the issue was sometimes contentious, but a majority of L&R members "saw that it is possible to both support people in their resistance, by opposing US military and economic domination, and to maintain a principled engagement with opposition movements that does not abdicate our responsibility to be critical of authoritarian practices and tendencies."

Debates inside L&R on questions of nationalism, anti-imperialism, and white-skin privilege crystallized at one point in a dispute about whether the group, which had always been overwhelmingly white, should attempt to transform itself into a "multiracial/multinational revolutionary anarchist organization." In an unsigned editorial from 1997, reprinted in the collection

A New World in Our Hearts, advocates of this position astutely
criticized the sort of solidarity model that May 19th helped pioneer:

> While we recognize the deep roots white supremacy has in the
> consciousness of most white people, we do not believe that only a
> handful of exemplary white people can be won to fighting white
> supremacy. We believe an end to this whole rotten system is in the
> ultimate interests of the vast majority of humanity, including
> the majority of white people. Accordingly, we reject the notion of
> the "white solidarity organization" that acts under the leadership
> of this or that people of color organization. The abdication [by]
> white people of the responsibility of thinking for themselves does not
> magically erase the colonial dynamic that exists between white
> people and people of color. The evasion of struggle over questions of
> principle for fear of being unpopular or criticized by people of color
> can only be called the politics of guilt. Moreover, the decision to take
> leadership from a particular organization is itself an intervention
> in the internal affairs of the community in which the organization is
> based. There is no escape from the logic of this society other than
> a revolutionary commitment to change it.

Going even further than the Sojourner Truth Organization,
L&R (or at least some of its members) highlighted many of the
same problems described in the present volume—abdication of
responsibility, politics of guilt, and the hypocrisy of pretending
that taking leadership is anything other than taking sides. Not
everyone in L&R agreed with this analysis, and the group collapsed
in 1998, unable to resolve multiple disagreements about the overall
viability of anarchism. In the intervening decades, anarchism as a
political approach has grown substantially in stature and influence

among organizers concentrating on racial justice. In this sense, it is clear that had L&R never existed, today's debates about allies and privilege would be framed in a much different way.

The Zapatista uprising in Chiapas, Mexico, that began on January 1, 1994, was possibly the most formative political experience for many members of L&R as well as an entire generation of radicals politicized between the fall of the Berlin Wall in 1989 and the attacks of September 11, 2001. The Ejercito Zapatista de Liberación Nacional (EZLN) presented itself to the world outside Chiapas in a way deliberately designed to draw in a wide range of supporters. This involved a fundamental reconceptualization of the idea of Third World solidarity into something perhaps more akin to the model of the original Rainbow Coalition.

The EZLN's charismatic spokesperson, Subcomandante Marcos, gave voice to this innovative solidarity model in an open letter a few months after the initial uprising. In a postscript to the 1994 "Communiqué about the End of the Consultations," inspired by government-sponsored attempts to malign him by speculating about his sexuality, he flipped the script, metaphorically embracing oppressed and marginalized people around the world:

> Marcos is gay in San Francisco, a black person in South Africa, Asian in Europe, a Chicano in San Isidro, an anarchist in Spain, a Palestinian in Israel, an Indigenous person in the streets of San Cristóbal, a gang-member in Neza, a rocker on [a university] campus, a Jew in Germany, an ombudsman in [the] Department of Defense, a feminist in a political party, a communist in the post–Cold War period, a prisoner in Cintalapa, a pacifist in Bosnia, a

Mapuche in the Andes, a teacher in [the] National Confederation of Educational Workers, an artist without a gallery or a portfolio, a housewife in any neighborhood in any city in any part of Mexico on a Saturday night, a guerrilla in Mexico at the end of the twentieth century, a striker in the CTM [Confederation of Mexican Workers], a sexist in the feminist movement, a woman alone in a Metro station at 10 p.m., a retired person standing around in the Zócalo, a campesino without land, an underground editor, an unemployed worker, a doctor with no office, a non-conformist student, a dissident against neoliberalism, a writer without books or readers, and a Zapatista in the Mexican Southeast. In other words, Marcos is a human being in this world. Marcos is every untolerated, oppressed, exploited minority that is resisting and saying, "Enough!" He is every minority who is now beginning to speak and every majority that must shut up and listen. He is every untolerated group searching for a way to speak, their way to speak. Everything that makes power and the good consciences of those in power uncomfortable—this is Marcos.

The breadth of common identity and struggle suggested by Marcos's statement was novel in a variety of ways. By highlighting so many different examples, it implicitly rejected any notion of hierarchies of oppression and privilege, and promoted ties of solidarity across the planet.

The unorthodox approach to solidarity taken by the EZLN bears some resemblance to the contemporary discourse of "intersectionality"—traditionally associated with black feminist arguments that race, class, and gender are inextricably connected in a broader system of oppression, and resistance must be similarly intertwined. As Thomas Olesen suggests in "Globalizing the

Zapatistas," the novelty of the Zapatistas is found in the ways in which their relationship with external solidarity groups "diverges significantly from the solidarity work of previous decades." He goes on to contend that

> had the Zapatistas limited themselves to the quest for indigenous autonomy, the transnational resonance would have been much less significant. The fundamental vision of the Zapatistas is, in other words, not to create a new identity or affirm an old identity in a negative manner by establishing a "them" and "us" dichotomy. The indigenous people and the Zapatistas are instead transformed into a universal symbol of exclusion and oppression. This is done in a way that invokes a global consciousness and opens the way to a solidarity allowing a variety of social struggles to articulate their particularity in a manner that simultaneously asserts and transcends identity.

The concept of asserting and transcending identity challenges much of the framework of today's ally politics. That Marcos was himself an outsider to the very struggle he helped lead—a privileged, urban, middle-class mestizo serving as the public face for a rural movement demanding indigenous autonomy—complicated things further. In contemporary parlance, Marcos-as-gay-in-San-Francisco is not entirely unlike a white person wearing an "I am Trayvon Martin" T-shirt at a protest against police brutality. If the symbolism is understood as an expression of solidarity rather than a false claim on an oppressed identity, we are more than partway to becoming accomplices.

The essays in this book share a conviction with the Zapatistas and the original Rainbow Coalition that political struggle is about building bridges. In the words of the EZLN, written in 2001, "Dignity is a bridge. It needs two sides that, being different, special, and distant, are united in the bridge without ceasing to be different and special, but ceasing to be distant." As the vignettes I've shared here indicate, bridge building can be messy; it will involve arguments and mistakes, but in the end, a willingness to learn the lessons of past efforts can make a real difference.

Read the essays here, then go back out there and keep on fighting. Keep on building bridges.

**Brave
Mother-
fuckers**

The
Poor
Person's

Defense
of Riots

The Poor Person's Defense of Riots: Practical Looting, Rational Riots, and the Shortcomings of Black Liberalism

This piece, following the Ferguson uprising, was written by **Delio Vasquez** and originally published with complete citations in *CounterPunch*, December 26, 2014.

On a warm night in December, over a thousand protesters find themselves trapped in a winding, residential area of Berkeley, surrounded on two sides by armed riot police. On the third side is a row of sleepy California homes. Opposite that is an empty parking lot surrounded by a chain-link fence. Some of the riot police lift and aim their rifles at the crowd, while other officers reach to have their plastic zip-tie cuffs at the ready. Realizing that there is no other way out, a handful of protesters, most of whom look like they came from poverty-stricken East Oakland rather than the collegiate suburbs of Berkeley, immediately know what to do. "Knock down the fence!" A horde of protesters rushes forward, pushing and pulling at the silver-painted fencing. Others, however, stand back. You can see the look of hesitation on the face of one dark-skinned woman. A young white male in an expensive-looking, untucked dress shirt shouts, "Hey guys, let's keep it nonviolent!" The police hesitate. After a collective effort, the protesters successfully manage to knock over the fence; they jump over a second smaller one, and most of them escape. A few stragglers aren't so lucky; one tall, African-American-looking man has his leg broken by a barrage of rubber bullets fired at close range and is soon arrested, despite the efforts of the crowd to protect him.

Since the Ferguson decision, we have been flooded with stories about how the overwhelmingly peaceful nationwide protests against police brutality have been occasionally ruined by looting and property destruction caused by "fringe" elements. In conservative media, the troublemakers have been generally characterized as parts of the black "criminal" underclass. In the liberal media, the lawbreakers have often been characterized as "outside agitators," "violent political radicals," and "white anarchists." While the conservative side has worked to make it seem like the actions of these black "criminals" are not legitimately political, the liberal side, on the other hand, has avoided publicizing stories about people of color engaging in property destruction altogether. There is a real danger that these omissions have been motivated by white guilt—as well as the legitimate concern that publicizing these stories will be interpreted as feeding into racism. Rather than challenging the assumption that property destruction is necessarily bad, however, many liberals have refused to acknowledge the lawbreaking altogether, perhaps for fear of being labeled racist.

Some of the more insightful attempts to defend rioting and property destruction in light of the history of US political dissent have unfortunately relied on moralistic arguments that portray rioting as driven primarily by emotion—with the idea being that we should sympathize with the feelings of the rioters. These stories reinforce the misconception that riots are all and only about anger, rage, and frustration. These perspectives also fail to acknowledge that when riots do happen, they arise from particular historical situations. It is not everyday oppression that immediately causes a riot but instead those symbolic events—like a major nonindictment—that shock the senses, shake our expectations, and act as a brutal affront to our collective sense of what is right (even if sometimes those expectations are sadly divorced from reality in the first place). Many times throughout history, populations have simply starved to death rather than riot; at other times they have rioted over matters that to us may seem less urgent. Accordingly, when someone takes the time to go smash a window, putting themselves in legal danger, we need to try to make sense of why they would do it.

Mob Decision Making

History shows us that mob actions are usually intentional, targeted, and quite often rational. During the eighteenth century, angry mobs of starving English peasants, rather than steal from grain merchants, forced them to sell the bread at a fair price decided by the crowd. In "The Moral Economy of the Crowd in the Eighteenth Century," E. P. Thompson cites the example of peasants "who, having taken corn from the farmers and [having] sold it at the popular price in the market, brought back to the farmers not only the money but also the sacks." In Ferguson, as noted in the *Jacobin Magazine* piece "In Defense of the Ferguson Riots," people have stopped in the middle of rioting to have impromptu theoretical discussions as well as strategically discuss, from the base of operations at a local gas station, where to target next. In Berkeley, corporate businesses like RadioShack, Wells Fargo, and Trader Joe's have been damaged and looted, but when individuals have chosen to break a residential window, collective boos and chants of

"No houses!" have risen from the crowd, and those individuals have been stopped without any further conflict.

Anyone who has been in a large crowd, be it a church group or political "mob," is well aware that spontaneous forms of group decision making often arise and allow the crowd to move with a more or less shared purpose. A form of group consciousness takes shape, with people communicating across the crowd to each other, protecting each other, and working together to avoid dangerous situations, such as being trapped by police maneuvers. Sometimes, too, there are bad forms of communication, and a crowd does not cooperate so well—but these communication failures are no less egregious than those that occur daily in the chambers of Congress, surely. Crowds make decisions together, and those decisions are cosigned by individuals who think through questions like, "Do I want to participate in this?" "Should I leave now or stay?" "Do I want to stand by and provide cover for those doing things that I refuse to do, or should I abandon them?"

When Smashing a Window Is "Just Political" and When It Is Practical

There is a stark difference between political protest and direct action. Political protest is a form of expression, done specifically so as to be seen by an audience—such as the general public or politicians in power—with the hope of convincing that audience to share the protesters' viewpoint and maybe act on their behalf. Direct action is also political, but avoids the "middleperson"; it is instead an action done to directly pursue a concrete goal, such as acquiring food with which to feed oneself. Holding a sign that criticizes Jim Crow laws is political protest; refusing to get off the bus or move to the back when ordered to is direct action. In *Race Rebels*, Robin Kelley explains how hundreds of individuals in the South were doing this before Rosa Parks and the NAACP successfully turned the act into an organized, political tactic. By the same token, Tea Partiers and conservatives who wave "Don't Tread on Me" flags are engaging in political protest; those who buy their own land and arm themselves to protect it are engaging in direct action.

The question, then, is when you smash a window, are you doing so because you are looking to grab some food or some diapers, or a television to sell so that you can make next month's rent? Or are you smashing a window to express anger and frustration, and so that maybe the elites or general public pay attention to your political views? If you are smashing a window for the second reason, you have more in common with those engaging in peaceful political protest. Both the person chanting "black lives matter" and the person putting up graffiti are engaging in political protest—to speak out against something.

By contrast, looting is rarely motivated purely by emotion or the desire for political expression, but instead must be more instrumental and practical than other forms of political action. Looting takes intentionality, foresight, and quick decision making, and directly results (unless you get arrested) in your acquiring the things that you are seeking. Because poor people often cannot afford to waste their time engaging in symbolic forms of protest, and because they rarely expect to be heard by those in power anyway, they are much more likely to engage in practical, direct action than in symbolic political protest. Things like stealing food from work, not paying taxes, and calling in sick to work when you're not actually sick are actions that produce clear results. By contrast, holding a sign and marching in circles for hours is admittedly a lot more abstract and requires free time that only some of us can afford. A mass "die-in" like those engaged in by many across the country is indubitably a valuable political action, but we would be deluding ourselves if we did not admit that the link between such symbolic acts and concrete political change can be painfully unclear and abstract, and the tactic slow moving in its effectiveness.

Black Liberalism and Disruptive Tactics

At a very large rally I recently attended in Oakland, several members of a coalitional group of black organizers spent a considerable amount of time laying out ground rules for reining in the voices of white "allies." The organizers argued that while well intentioned, white allies often reinforce racism by taking over political demonstrations that are about issues that black people face. Most white participants that I observed were willing to accept these critiques, deferring to what they felt was the greater authority that the black leadership should rightfully have over a movement that involves most prominently the deaths and abuses of black persons. The rally then turned into what was essentially a passive crowd listening to and watching a black leadership give speeches from the steps of the Alameda County Courthouse. Some in the audience took group photos and selfies of themselves with the black leadership in the background, feeling that they had performed well as silent, white allies, and went home with smiles on their faces. As I later found out, many of those black leaders later met at an exclusive cocktail party scheduled for that evening. At the same time that the party was happening, about a thousand people of mixed racial and class backgrounds continued in the streets, after the "official" rally had ended, marching and demonstrating for the next few hours and blocking a major traffic tunnel; some of them ended up getting tased and beaten by police, and many others were arrested.

While the black critique of overzealous white allies may seem like a positive intervention to limit racism, it can instead frequently become a way for self-designated "black leaders"—who also happen to be more moderate—to successfully demobilize and marginalize the more disruptive branches of a movement, shaming white radicals through white guilt while also making it seem like the more radical organizers of color and poor people who have come to protest simply do not exist. Often, these black moderates and liberals focus their attention on intramovement racism and "microaggressions" because the more brutal dimensions of racism specific to poverty, like intense police violence, may in fact be outside their lived experiences. Sometimes, middle- and upper-class people of color who have not actually experienced severe police brutality can only understand racism through their experiences of subtler structural forms of racism, like discriminatory hiring practices or racially insensitive language. To them, the unarguably racist tones of a "white radical" who disagrees with moderate strategies and tactlessly insults a black liberal leader are easier to address, more tempting to attack, and simply more familiar than the racist violence that poor people of color experience.

Of course, affluent people of color experience police violence as well. As Dr. Ersula Ore and Dr. Henry Louis Gates know well, rarely will police stop to take note of how many degrees you may have, how "respectable" you may be, or even if you happen to be an off-duty police officer yourself. But these experiences simply cannot be equated with the constant threats of violent death and malnutrition that poor people of color face on a daily basis. The failure to acknowledge these class differences then means that black liberals and moderates gloss over the crucial fact that many of the poor people who have been most brutally abused by police in the past turn out to be the same people who later decide to engage in looting. Accordingly, when the president talks about his struggles catching cabs in Chicago or being confused for a waiter, only to then turn around and insist to us that we must accept the decisions made by the grand jury and trust "the rule of law," despite overwhelming evidence that the institutions of law—the police, the justice system, and so on—are the very problem that people are protesting against, it becomes hard to ignore that notwithstanding the racism that the president has faced, he likely cannot relate to the forms of racism that someone like Michael Brown experienced.

A History of Lawbreaking

We often suffer from a collective amnesia about the crucial role of lawbreaking in the history of social change. Martin Luther King Jr., the paragon of pacifist protest, was arrested an impressive thirty times between 1955 and 1965. And still, the effectiveness of his militant pacifism can only be properly understood against the background of many other, much more tumultuous political conflicts—riots included—that occurred throughout the civil rights movement. Political change does not, and never has, come about through peaceful protest alone. All tactics of course play a role—and riots, the threat of violence, and violence itself are frequently the context and background that situate as well as frame the force and effectiveness of more mainstream, moderate, and agreed-on tactics. In a conversation with Coretta Scott King, Malcolm X, infamous for his antipacifist rhetoric and direct attacks on Martin Luther King's strategies, nonetheless stressed to King's wife his awareness of the value of a diversity of tactics: "I want Dr. King to know that I didn't come to Selma to make his job difficult. I really did come thinking I could make it easier. If the white people realize what the alternative is, perhaps they will be more willing to hear Dr. King."

Ultimately, then, we do ourselves a disservice when we attack others for doing the important political work that we ourselves are not willing to do—work that in fact allows us to do what we do. As a political theorist, I do not have the patience to research the various ways and tedious details that show how procedural corruption may have occurred during the Michael Brown case, but I appreciate the contributions of the lawyers and legal experts who do that important work. Equally, those who work inside formal institutions to pass antipolice brutality policy and legislation must also acknowledge that their voices would not be heard were it not for the background roar of those angry mobs shouting outside our legislative buildings and in the streets.

The Poor Person's Defense of Riots

Decolonize

Together

Decolonize Together:
Moving beyond a Politics of Solidarity toward a Practice of Decolonization

Different versions of this piece by **Harsha Walia** have appeared in *Briarpatch* magazine and the anthology *Organize! Building from the Local for Global Justice*. This version is from the blog Unsettling America: Decolonization in Theory and Practice, https://unsettlingamerica.wordpress.com.

North America's state and corporate wealth is largely based on the subsidies provided by the theft of indigenous lands and resources. Colonial conquest was designed to ensure the forced displacement of indigenous peoples from their territories, destruction of autonomy and self-determination in indigenous self-governance, and assimilation of indigenous peoples' cultures and traditions. Given the devastating cultural, spiritual, economic, linguistic, and political impacts on indigenous people, any serious social or environmental justice movement must necessarily include nonnative solidarity in the fight against colonization.

Decolonization is as much a process as a goal. It requires a profound re-centering of indigenous worldviews in our movements for political liberation, social transformation, renewed cultural kinships, and the development of an economic system that serves rather than threatens our collective life on this planet. As stated by Toronto-based activist Syed Hussan, "Decolonization is a dramatic re-imagining of relationships with land, people and the state. Much of this requires study, it requires conversation, it is a practice, it is an unlearning."

It is a positive sign that a growing number of social movements are recognizing that indigenous self-determination must become the foundation for all our broader social justice mobilizing. Indigenous peoples are the most impacted by the pillage of lands, experience disproportionate poverty and homelessness, are overrepresented in statistics of missing and murdered women, and are the primary targets of repressive policing and prosecutions in the criminal injustice system. Rather than being treated as a single issue within a laundry list of demands, indigenous self-determination is increasingly understood as intertwined with struggles against racism, poverty, police violence, war and occupation, violence against women, and environmental justice.

Intersectional approaches can, however, subordinate and compartmentalize indigenous struggle within the machinery of existing leftist narratives: anarchists point to the antiauthoritarian tendencies within indigenous communities, environmentalists highlight the connection to land that indigenous communities have, antiracists subsume indigenous people into the broader discourse about systemic oppression, and women's organizations point to relentless violence borne by indigenous women in discussions about patriarchy.

We have to be cautious to avoid replicating the state's assimilationist model of liberal pluralism, whereby indigenous identities are forced to fit within our existing groups and narratives. The inherent right to traditional lands and self-determination is expressed collectively, and should not be subsumed within the discourse of individual or human rights. Furthermore, it is imperative to understand being indigenous as not just an identity but rather a way of life, which is intricately connected to indigenous people's relationship to the land and all its inhabitants. Indigenous struggle cannot simply be accommodated within other struggles; it demands solidarity on its own terms.

The Practice of Solidarity

One of the basic principles of indigenous solidarity organizing is the notion of taking leadership. According to this principle, nonnatives must be accountable and responsive to the experiences, voices, needs, and political perspectives of indigenous people themselves. From an anti-oppression perspective, nonnatives cannot direct meaningful support for indigenous struggles. Taking leadership means being humble and honoring frontline voices of resistance as well as offering tangible solidarity as needed and requested. Specifically, this translates to taking initiative for self-education about the specific histories of the lands we reside on, organizing support with the clear guidance and consent of an indigenous community or group, building long-term relationships of accountability, and never assuming or taking for granted the personal and political trust that nonnatives may earn from indigenous peoples over time.

In offering support to a specific community in their struggle, nonnatives should organize with a mandate from the community and understanding of the parameters of the support that is being sought. Once these guidelines are established, nonnatives should be proactive in offering logistic, fund-raising, and campaign support. Clear lines of communication must be maintained and a commitment made for long-term support. This means that activists should not just be present for blockades or in moments of crisis but instead sustain a multiplicity of meaningful and diverse relationships on an ongoing basis. Feminist writer bell hooks suggests, "Solidarity is not the same as support. To experience solidarity, we must have a community of interests, shared beliefs and goals around which to unite, to build Sisterhood. Support can be occasional. It can be given and just as easily withdrawn. Solidarity requires sustained, ongoing commitment."

Organizing in accordance with these principles is not always straightforward. Respecting indigenous leadership is not the same as waiting around to be told what to do while you do nothing. "I am waiting to be told exactly what to do" should not be an excuse for inaction, and seeking guidance must be weighed against the possibility of further burdening indigenous people with questions. The appropriate line between being too interventionist and being paralyzed will be aided by a willingness to decenter oneself, and learning and acting from a place of responsibility rather than guilt.

Cultivating an ethic of responsibility begins with nonnatives understanding ourselves as beneficiaries of the illegal settlement of indigenous people's land, and unjust appropriation of indigenous peoples' resources and jurisdiction. When faced with this truth, it is common for activists to get stuck in their feelings of guilt, which I would argue is a state of self-absorption that actually upholds privilege. While guilt is often representative of a much-needed shift in consciousness, in itself it does nothing to motivate the responsibility necessary to actively dismantle entrenched systems of oppression. In a movement-building round table, longtime Montreal activist Jaggi Singh expressed that "the only way to escape complicity with settlement is active opposition to it. That only happens in the context of on-the-ground, day-to-day organizing, and creating and cultivating the spaces where we can begin dialogues and discussions as natives and nonnatives."

Alliances with indigenous communities should be based on shared values, principles, and analysis. For example, during the anti-Olympics campaign in 2010, activists chose not to align with the Four Host First Nations, a pro-corporate body created in conjunction with the Vancouver Olympics Organizing Committee. Instead, we took leadership from and strengthened alliances with land defenders in the Secwepemc and St'át'imc nations as well as indigenous people being directly impacted by homelessness and poverty in the Downtown Eastside. In general, however, differences surrounding strategy within a community should be for community members to discuss and resolve. We should be cautious of a persistent dynamic where solidarity activists start to fixate on the internal politics of an oppressed community. Allies should avoid trying to intrude and interfere in struggles within and between a community, which perpetuates the civilizing ideology of the white man's burden and violates the basic principles of self-determination.

Building intentional alliances should also avoid devolution into tokenization. Nonnatives often determine which indigenous voices to privilege by defaulting to the more "well-known," "easy to get ahold of," or "less hostile" indigenous activists. This selectivity distorts the diversity present in indigenous communities, and can exacerbate tensions and colonially imposed divisions between indigenous peoples. In opposing the colonialism of the state and settler society, nonnatives must recognize our own role in perpetuating colonialism within our solidarity efforts. We actively counter this by theorizing and discussing the nuanced issues of solidarity, leadership, strategy, and analysis not in abstraction but instead within our real, informed, and sustained relationships with indigenous peoples.

Decolonizing Relationships

While centering and honoring indigenous voices and leadership, the obligation for decolonization does rest on all of us. As written by Nora Butler Burke in "Building a 'Canadian' Decolonization Movement: Fighting the Occupation at 'Home,'" "A decolonisation movement cannot be comprised solely of solidarity and support for Indigenous peoples' sovereignty and self-determination. If we are in support of self-determination, we too need to be self-determining. It is time to cut the state out of this relationship, and to replace it with a new relationship, one which is mutually negotiated, and premised on a core respect for autonomy and freedom."

Being responsible for decolonization often requires us to locate ourselves within the context of colonization in complicated ways—frequently as simultaneously oppressed and complicit. This is true, for example, for racialized migrants in Canada. Within the anticolonial migrant justice movement of No One Is Illegal, we go beyond demanding citizenship rights for racialized migrants as that would lend false legitimacy to a settler state. We challenge the official state discourse of multiculturalism that undermines the autonomy of indigenous communities by granting and mediating rights through the imposed structures of the state, and seeks to assimilate diversities into a singular Canadian identity. Anticolonial feminist Andrea Smith reminds us that "all non-Native peoples are promised the ability to join in the colonial project of settling indigenous lands. ... In all of these cases, we would check our aspirations against the aspirations of other communities to ensure that our model of liberation does not become the model of oppression for others." In British Columbia, immigrants and refugees have participated in several delegations to indigenous blockades, while indigenous communities have offered protection and refuge for migrants facing deportation.

Decolonization is the process whereby we intend the conditions we want to live and social relations we wish to have. We have to supplant the colonial logic of the state itself. German philosopher Gustav Landauer wrote almost a hundred years ago that "the State is a condition, a certain relationship between human beings, a mode of behaviour; we destroy it by contracting other relationships." Decolonization requires us to exercise our sovereignties differently, and reconfigure our communities based on shared experiences, ideals, and visions. Almost all indigenous formulations of sovereignty—such as the Two Row Wampum agreement of peace, friendship, and respect between the Haudenosaunee nations and settlers—are premised on revolutionary notions of respectful coexistence and stewardship of the land, which goes far beyond any Western liberal democratic ideal.

I have been encouraged to think of human interconnectedness and kinship in building alliances with indigenous communities. Black/Cherokee writer Zainab Amadahy uses the term "Relationship Framework" to describe how our activism should be grounded: "Understanding the world through a Relationship Framework, where we don't see ourselves, our communities, or our species as inherently superior to any other, but rather see our roles and responsibilities to each other as inherent to enjoying our life experiences." Striving toward decolonization and walking together toward transformation requires us to challenge a dehumanizing social organization that perpetuates our isolation from each other, and normalizes a lack of responsibility to one another and the earth.

Dangerous
Allies

Dangerous Allies

Tipu's Tiger, a writing collective, offers new material here along with revised excerpts from its April 2012 pamphlet "Who Is Oakland," about the racial politics of Occupy Oakland and its critics.

This essay is offered in deep solidarity with anyone committed to ending oppression and exploitation materially. By using the term "materially," we simply mean that we view patriarchy, class war, antiblackness, and anti-immigrant racism not only in terms of individual prejudice or pathology but also as structural consequences of national borders, capitalist economies, state policies, and long histories of black slavery, segregation, and colonialism.

While twenty-first-century anti-oppression politics in the United States is an evolving patchwork of theories and practices, we believe in the necessity of identity-based organizing, and the need for political campaigns to be led by groups directly impacted by specific forms of oppression and exploitation. At the same time, we have witnessed how dominant forms of anti-oppression activism continue to promote two strategically disastrous assumptions: that racial justice is achieved through the redistribution of racial privilege, and that identity categories describe homogeneous communities made up of individuals with identical political agendas.

With the power to define the role of the "good ally" and "outside agitator" in antiracist struggles, liberal activist groups have become a key component of counterinsurgency campaigns conducted against a range of recent social movements from Occupy to Black Lives Matter. In the Black Lives Matter movement in particular, police chiefs and municipal politicians across the United States have drawn on the language of community to marginalize and discredit radical black perspectives, and displace militant action onto white outsiders.

We reject a politics that takes as its ultimate goal the redistribution of something like white privilege rather than its elimination and the radical transformation of the structures that produce that privilege in the first place. But we also reject a number of recent critiques of the politics of privilege—often used to dismiss feminist, antiracist, and queer analysis and organizing—which simply refuse to understand privilege as a consequence of deep material divisions within coalitional identities like the "99%."

According to the dominant discourse of "white privilege," for example, white supremacy is primarily a psychological attitude that individuals can voluntarily choose to relinquish as opposed to a set of institutional arrangements producing antiblack, anti-immigrant, and anti-Muslim violence at the level of entire populations—from policing, prisons, housing, and health care, to labor markets, workplaces, border militarization, and the "War on Terror."

The politics of privilege has consistently been invoked to demonize confrontational street tactics. Until the recent wave of revolts that have erupted across the United States in response to antiblack police violence, liberal activist groups have consistently condemned disruptive protests—from marching without permits to blocking traffic on roads and highways—as just so many examples of white privilege.

Instead, contemporary social justice activism has historically imagined the solution to the problem of privilege as state-, corporate-, or nonprofit-managed racial and ethnic diversity within existing hierarchies of power. It is a well-worn activist formula to point out that oppressed groups must be placed front and center in struggles against racism, sexism, and homophobia. US social movements are now operating in a political environment where demands for racial justice have been translated into inclusion within oppressive systems—where the US Border Patrol is 54 percent Latino/a, where the percentage of nonwhite police officers working in US law enforcement has almost doubled from 1987 to 2013, and where the US Army is simultaneously one of the most racially integrated and oppressive institutions in the world. Police chiefs, politicians, business interests, and even many progressive activists have strategically invoked the language of "community" to bring protests under control. The complex interplay of race, gender, sexuality, and class do not automatically create a shared political vision, even though it may create a shared sense of oppression and linked fate among a people. Identity does not automatically mean solidarity. But the uneven impact of identity-based oppression across society creates the conditions for the emergence of autonomous groups organizing on the basis of a common political understanding of those experiences.

Identity Is Not Solidarity

The politics of privilege and the conservative appropriation of the language of community have ended up reinforcing racial stereotypes about the political homogeneity and helplessness of "communities of color." The category "people of color" is itself a recently invented identity category that obscures the central role that antiblackness plays in maintaining the US racial order while concealing nonwhite interracial conflict.

Time and again politicians have betrayed the very racial and ethnic groups they belong to and claim to represent, while also being held up as proof that the United States is indeed a color-blind or postracial society. At the same time, the nation as a whole has returned to levels of racial inequality as well as residential and educational segregation unseen since the last so-called postracial moment in US history—the mid-1960s' legal repeal of the apartheid system of Jim Crow.

Wealthy queers support initiatives that lock up and murder poor queers, trans* people, and sex workers. Women in positions of power continue to defend and sometimes initiate the vicious assault on abortion and reproductive rights, and then off-load reproductive labor onto the shoulders of care workers, who are predominantly women of color whose employment is often directly tied to their citizenship status. The politics of "leaning in" for a small layer of wealthy women has dovetailed with budget cuts and health care rollbacks that have left poor women at the mercy of misogynist, increasingly lethal anti-reproductive-rights legislation, and left poor, queer and trans* people without access to necessary medical resources like hormones or AIDS medication.

But more pertinent for our argument is the phenomenon of anti-oppression activists—who *do* advance a structural analysis of oppression, and yet consistently align themselves with a praxis that reduces the history of violent and radically unsafe antislavery, anticolonial, antipatriarchal, antihomophobic, and anti-ciscentric freedom struggles to current campaigns for increased electoral representation or symbolic inclusion. Even when these activists invoke a history of militant resistance and sacrifice, they consistently fall back on strategies of petitioning the powerful to renounce their privilege and support individuals from marginalized populations only when they do the same.

Rejecting this liberal political framework has become synonymous with a refusal to seriously address racism, sexism, and homophobia in general. Even and especially when nonwhite people, women, and queers imagine and execute alternatives to this liberal politics of cultural inclusion, they are persistently attacked as white, male, and privileged by the cohort that maintains and perpetuates the dominant praxis.

Race Leaders and Legitimate Protest

A vast nonprofit-industrial complex and elite racial leadership class has arisen since the 1960s to define the parameters of acceptable political action and debate. As riots and rebellions return to the United States, the dominant praxis of contemporary anti-oppression politics has largely refused to question the alienated governance structures that create the need for "race leaders" in the first place rather than already-existing popular assemblies and other forms of decentralized decision making, within and when needed, between groups directly impacted by antiblack state violence, rape and sexual assault, deportations, surveillance, and extreme racial inequality.[1]

Dangerous Allies

When activists claim that poor black and brown communities must not defend themselves against racist attacks or state violence, especially not through the use of illegal tactics, they typically advocate instead the performance of an image of "legitimate" victimhood for white middle-class consumption. "Communities of color" have become in contemporary liberal anti-oppression discourse akin to endangered species in need of management by sympathetic whites or community leaders assigned to contain political conflict at all costs.

Echoing right-wing racist rhetoric, liberal organizations routinely smear "illegitimate," nonpacifist resistance as senseless and the work of irrational "thugs." And yet it is precisely marginalized groups utilizing these tactics—poor women of color defending their right to land and housing; trans* street workers and indigenous peoples fighting back against murder and violence; black and brown struggles against white supremacist violence—that have waged the most powerful and successful uprisings in US history. It is extremely advantageous to the powers that be for these groups to be deterred from the risks of militant self-defense, resistance, or attack. We refuse a politics that infantilizes nonwhite and/or nonmale groups, and believes that they are incapable of fighting for their own liberation, as the old saying goes, by any means necessary.

Defining the Good Ally

Who is a social justice ally? As a recent article from the xBorder Collective observes, the concept of allyship has been largely defined by social justice organizations in terms of the relative privilege of outsiders looking to support the political struggles of groups to which they do not belong:

> The theory of the ally in this sense examines and expands upon issues relating to the role of men with respect to feminist struggle, white people with respect to anti-racist struggle, etc. Much of the discussion and debate within this discourse turns on the question of the "good" ally, of how a person of privilege committed to ally work must acknowledge and reflect upon their privileges and do the intellectual and practical work to divest themselves of the illegitimate power such privilege affords. These discussions may be directed at a generalized

concept of, e.g., the white anti-racist ally as well as questions of what it means to develop specific and personal relations of trust between individuals and groups involved in anti-oppression work. This conception of the ally calls to attention the place of power within relationships, structures, practices and processes, not simply the content of particular demands or objectives.

The theory of allyship offered here would seem to be informed by a genuine desire to follow the lead of communities in struggle while remaining ethically accountable to these groups. By respecting the experiential knowledge and tactical intelligence of groups directly impacted by specific forms of oppression, good allies would in theory remain attentive to forms of power, prejudice, and ignorance that reproduce oppressive dynamics within activist spaces.

And yet as the Black Lives Matter movement has unfolded, the concept of allyship has been repeatedly mobilized in practice to oppose almost every action that helped the movement expand beyond the control of police chiefs and municipal politicians across the United States. Apparently unaware of the irony of denouncing "out-of-state activists" while quoting Martin Luther King Jr., activists who identify with the politics of white allyship have consistently condemned escalating protests from Ferguson to Baltimore and the Bay Area for rejecting pacifism, and instead answering police murder with flames, riots, and rocks. Literally policing the boundaries of acceptable protest, self-identified white allies have even physically fought black, brown, and other protesters in the streets of Oakland and Berkeley in order to protect businesses like RadioShack and prevent dumpsters from being set on fire.

These antiracist movement experts and peacekeepers could only exist in an age when massive upheavals like Watts in 1965 and the Detroit Rebellions of 1967 have been pathologized and then erased from public memory. Because of the return of this defiance to US streets, many who would otherwise ignore the ongoing police murders of black people won't easily forget Oscar Grant, Trayvon Martin, Rekia Boyd, Renisha McBride, Michael Brown, Eric Garner, and Freddie Gray, among countless others.

But what looks like discrepancy between theory and practice is in fact a consistent application of the basic principles of allyship developed within conservative institutional contexts in the aftermath of 1960s-era movements of black liberation. As black and brown militants at the time were incarcerated, killed, or driven underground, remaining movement activists entered educational institutions and electoral politics, with a small leadership class becoming integrated into the vast patronage networks of city and state governments.[2] It is within the context of increasingly institutionally funded, electorally oriented social justice campaigns—institutional groups that have tried to de-escalate popular mobilizations in Ferguson, for example—that the concept of the ally has been defined.[3] This is the shifting multiracial terrain on which the Black Lives Matter movement has fought both its enemies and peacekeeping "allies" in cities and towns across the nation.

The concept of allyship has been mobilized and defined strategically by a range of self-identified leaders and organizations in the Black Lives Matter movement. But this is where ally politics confronts a fundamental contradiction: black people in the United States hold different, frequently opposed political beliefs about effective movement strategy and tactics. Liberal ally politics can end up imposing inadvertently racist assumptions about the political homogeneity of racial and ethnic groups.

Precisely because there is not one but instead many often-irreconcilable visions of antiracist, feminist, and queer liberation along with a myriad of competing activist groups, being a "good ally" has relied on the concept of privilege as a substitute for critical assessment of the specific content of various political programs and objectives. In practice, allyship has taken the form of following self-identified leaders of oppressed groups whose political prescriptions are frequently based on a dismissal of tactical escalation as expressions of privilege.

The concept of allyship has been instrumental in imposing more moderate power brokers and elite protest managers on decentralized movements in an attempt to rein in disruptive protest. Any social movement in recent memory that has attempted to break the mold of permitted rallies and marches, and raise the economic cost of doing business as usual, has had to face a social justice industry designed to channel social unrest back into electoral politics, elite representation, and fantasies of political reform without mass popular resistance.[4] When actions are not organized and led by a recognizable coalition of vetted political organizations typically under the umbrella of the Democratic Party—or in other words, when young black movement participants in places like Baltimore have acted outside the system of formal political representation—self-proclaimed leaders and their allies have declared these actions illegitimate or the work of outsiders.[5]

"Outside Agitators" and "Thugs" in the Black Lives Matter Movement

So it has been predictable to witness once again domestic efforts to contain the Black Lives Matter movement by recycling language deployed against 1960s-era civil rights activists by cynically blaming "outside agitators" for diluting the message of "legitimate" protesters. The image of the outside agitator has remained a brutally effective part of counterinsurgency campaigns mounted against a range of recent social movements by liberal activist organizations from MoveOn.org to Al Sharpton's National Action Network.

Both the figure of the ally and outside agitator have been consistently invoked to exclude black, brown, and other radical voices from social movements, and demonize militant action through sanitized, historically inaccurate references to the civil rights movement.[6] When it became clear that outsiders were not responsible for increasingly fierce resistance in Baltimore after the police murder of Freddie Gray, for instance, Baltimore Democratic mayor Stephanie Rawlings-Blake called protesters "thugs" before instituting a citywide curfew in addition to an already-existing daytime curfew for minors.

"Occupy" versus "Decolonize"

In one particularly stark example of translating political debates into the language of privilege, at the December 4, 2011, Occupy Oakland general assembly, "white allies" from a local social justice nonprofit called the Catalyst Project arrived with an array of other groups and individuals to Oscar Grant / Frank Ogawa Plaza in order to speak in favor of a proposal to rename Occupy Oakland as "Decolonize / Liberate Oakland."[7] Speaking to the audience as though it were homogeneously white, each white ally who addressed the general assembly explained that renouncing their own white privilege meant supporting the renaming proposal.

And yet in the public responses to the proposal, it became clear that a substantial number of nonwhite people in the audience, including the founders of an Occupy Oakland black direct action group, the Tactical Action Committee, completely opposed the measure. As the meeting went on, it became apparent that for many participants, the language of decolonization, while appropriate to indigenous struggles, didn't seem to accurately describe the situation of black Oakland residents.

What was at stake was a political disagreement—one that was not clearly divided along racial lines. The failure of the renaming proposal, however, was subsequently widely misrepresented as a conflict between "white Occupy" and the "Decolonize / Liberate Oakland" group. In our experience, such misrepresentations are not accidental or isolated incidents but rather a repeated feature of a dominant strain of anti-oppression politics that—instead of mobilizing nonwhite people, women, trans* people, queers, and other oppressed people for independent action—has consistently erased the presence of more militant nonwhite people who have planned and participated in anticapitalist, anticolonial, black liberation, and antiauthoritarian movements.

Increasing the racial diversity of its personnel will not reform the structurally racist institutions of US policing. White supremacy will not be dismantled by sympathetic white activists spending several thousand dollars for nonprofit diversity trainings that can assist them in recognizing their own racial privilege and certifying their decision to do so. The absurdity of privilege politics re-centers antiracist practice on whites and white guilt, and assumes that antiblack racism (and by implicit or explicit association, misogyny, homophobia, and transphobia) manifests primarily as individual privileges that can be "checked" or dissolved through confessions of complicity in activist spaces while at the same time these so-called allies denounce militancy in the streets.

The riots, blockades, fires, and refusals to disperse in Ferguson, Baltimore, and countless other cities across the United States have presented a radical challenge to this failed, stagnant model of social change. Imagining alternatives to contemporary ally politics might begin by acknowledging that social movements do not speak with a single voice, and that despite shared identities, movement participants are committed to divergent aims, and sometimes directly opposed strategies and tactics. Who we choose to support and remain accountable to within oppressed groups is an unavoidably political decision that cannot be decided on the basis of identity alone.

Militant Black Lives Matter protests in Ferguson and Baltimore, for example, have come into direct conflict with police chiefs and officers, mayors, city politicians, businesspeople, and journalists—whose jobs depend on co-opting or crushing dissent within the communities they claim to represent. This means that outsiders who wish to support these movements must do the difficult work of navigating between a recognition of the ways in which their material position in society makes it difficult for them to understand the struggles and experiences of others, and an active assessment of a political landscape in which identity does not mean solidarity.

The Necessity of Autonomous Organizing

To attack a system that has evolved to contain social movements through elite representation, we believe in the absolute necessity of autonomous organizing. By "autonomous," we mean the formation of independent groups of people who face specific forms of exploitation and oppression, including but not limited to nonwhite people, women, indigenous people, nonwhite and white queers, people with disabilities, trans* and gender-nonconforming people, and the poor. Creating a variety of spaces as free from antiblackness, racism, sexism, and sexual violence as possible are the minimal conditions needed for political projects to survive over time. We also believe in the political value of organizing across social divisions with the understanding that any identity category is already a "coalition" of different groups with often radically different political interests depending on the issues being addressed.

We hope for the emergence of widespread autonomous organizing. We believe that a future beyond the histories of enslavement, colonization, and genocide of non-European populations that produced the conditions for the emergence of global capitalism—and beyond the many thousand years of violent patriarchal structuring of society along hierarchized and increasingly binary gender lines—will require revolutions within revolutions. Capitalism's ecocidal destiny, and its relentless global production of poverty, misery, abuse, and disposable and enslavable populations, will force increasingly catastrophic social change within most of our lifetimes—whether US social movements can meet the challenge or not.

No individual or single organization can speak for nonwhite people, women, the world's colonized populations, workers, or any demographic category as a whole—although nonwhite, female and queer, and labor activists from the Global North routinely and arrogantly claim this right.

Black liberation, civil rights, feminist, labor, and decolonization struggles clearly reveal that if resistance is even slightly effective, *the people who struggle are in danger.* The choice is not between danger and safety but rather between the uncertain dangers of revolt and the certainty of a world with no future.

Notes

1   On the historically "counterrevolutionary" role of the black leadership class during Reconstruction, the civil rights movement, and as a tool of indirect colonial rule in Africa—and on the more radical alternative of mass participatory politics promoted by civil rights activists like Fannie Lou Hamer—see R. L. Stephens II, "Dear #BlackLivesMatter: We Don't Need Black Leadership," Orchestrated Pulse blog, http://www.orchestratedpulse.com/2015/08/black-lives-matter-leadership/ (accessed August 15, 2105).

2   For a history of the institutional incorporation and increasing conservatism of 1960s-era black freedom struggles, see Cedric Johnson, *Revolutionaries to Race Leaders: Black Power and the Making of African American Politics* (Minneapolis: University of Minnesota Press, 2007).

3   For an account of pre-verdict preparations to de-escalate conflict and work with authorities to flag "troublesome individuals" in the Ferguson protests, see Carimah Townes, "With Grand Jury Decision Imminent, Clergy in Ferguson Step Up as Peacekeepers," ThinkProgress RSS, November 12, 2014.

4   For an analysis of why mass defiant behavior—like riots, illegal strikes, and street battles with the police—are not seen as political action at all by academics, activists, and media commentators, see Frances Fox Piven and Richard A. Cloward, "Poor People's Movements and the Structuring of Protest," *Poor People's Movements: Why They Succeed, How They Fail* (New York: Pantheon, 1977), 1–37.

5   For an account of failed attempts by local clergy to manage protests in Ferguson, see, for example, Jeff Hood, "The Violence of Demanding Peaceful Protest: The Missteps of Clergy in Ferguson," HuffingtonPost.com, August 24, 2014.

6   It is in this political climate that professional activist groups have abandoned the "resistance" in "nonviolent resistance" in favor of the theatrical performance of pacifism. On the strategic role of armed self-defense in the civil rights movement, see Akinyele Omowale Umoja, *We Will Shoot Back: Armed Resistance in the Mississippi Freedom Movement* (New York: New York University Press, 2013); Charles E. Cobb Jr., *This Nonviolent Stuff'll Get You Killed: How Guns Made the Civil Rights Movement Possible* (New York: Basic Books, 2014). For an overview of recent references to civil rights history in the context of the Black Lives Matter movement, see Lorenzo St. Dubois, "Misunderstanding the Civil Rights Movement and Diversity of Tactics," Diversity of Tactics blog, https://tacticaldiversity.wordpress.com/2015/05/28/misunderstanding-the-civil-rights-movement-and-diversity-of-tactics/ (accessed August 15, 2015).

7   For another account of this assembly, see Jaime Yassin, "Word versus Action," Hyphenated-Republic blog, https://hyphenatedrepublic.wordpress.com/2011/12/05/word-versus-action/ (accessed June 20, 2015).

A Critique

of
Ally

Politics

A Critique of Ally Politics

This piece emerged from reflections on recent struggles in
Durham, North Carolina, and was originally published as a zine
in 2013 under the title "Ain't No PC Gonna Fix It, Baby."
Its author, **M.**, can be reached at sweet_things@riseup.net.

Dear Beloved Ones in Struggle,

This essay is a love letter to you because I believe in our
tremendous power together. I have felt the powers over us, the
authorities who would be, *tremble*, when we can find each other in
real and lasting ways. I want to talk survival/liberation with
you because those two ideas are inextricably intertwined, as is my
future to yours.

We have a lot of work to do checking our egos, while
bringing up our fighting spirit and balancing it with wisdom.
Immersed in endless disappointing and hurtful experiences with
friends, comrades, and activists, my need is unrelenting for us to
practically rethink how we engage with the question of otherness
and the organization of our lives. How do we integrate a genuine
approach to anti-oppression? It's painfully clear that spitefully
throwing out all frameworks of understanding oppression as a
response to critiquing ally politics only works to destroy us. This
writing takes apart the concept of "ally" in political work with a
focus on race, though clearly there are parallels through and across
other experiences of identity.

I want to recognize that the stories told here are missing much of their complexity and nuance because of limited time and space, but I'm using them to highlight a few dynamics that I've seen consistently replicated in a wide variety of situations. Please talk about it with each other, share your thoughts and stories together, and give me constructive criticism if you want. I hope you feel it.

Allyship as Identity

The liberal concept of allyship is embedded in a rights-based discourse of identity politics. It works with the ideas that there are fixed groups of people (black people, women, gay people, and so on) that have been wronged by the structural oppressions of our society, that we must work across these differences to achieve equality for all, and that this responsibility falls especially on those who most benefit from structural oppressions. It centers on the idea that everyone has different life experiences that are shaped by our perceived identities, and so if you have an identity that is privileged in our society, you cannot understand the experiences of someone with an identity that is oppressed.

According to ally politics, in order to undermine whatever social privileges you benefit from, you must give up your role as a primary actor and become an ally to the oppressed. A good ally learns that if you can never understand the implications of walking through this world as an oppressed [fill in the blank with a person on the receiving end of a specific oppression], the only way to act with integrity is to follow the leadership of those who are oppressed in that way, support their projects and goals, and always seek out their suggestions and listen to their ideas when you are not sure what to do next.

It starts to get real complicated, real fast, however, as you discover that there is no singular mass of people of color—or any other identity-based group—to take guidance from, and that people within a single identity will not only disagree about important things but also will often have directly conflicting desires.

I lived for a short while in a historically black neighborhood that was increasingly becoming comprised of Latino families, college kids, and other (mostly working-class) renters.[1] I made friends swiftly with my neighbors—black elders who remembered when the road was gravel and gifted me with endless hours sitting on the porch telling their stories, Latino families that moved in to rent at the same time I did, and young black families with raucous teenagers who I'd run into on the street at all hours of the day and night. The neighborhood was alive with music and gardens, cookouts and camaraderie—and it was also engaged in a fierce battle against gentrification.

A condo development at the top of my street threatened the neighborhood's existence—and the development actually acknowledged that fact by promising to include a history of the soon-to-be wrecked neighborhood in its expensive courtyard. Wanting to better understand the political terrain of this project, I went to a neighborhood association meeting advertising an important discussion about it. With maybe a dozen people in attendance, I was the only renter, three-quarters of the people were white, and there were three cops. Before the meeting, I had wondered why none of the advertisements were bilingual and there was no option for Spanish-to-English translation, when so many of my adult neighbors weren't fluent in English. At the meeting, it was clear that assembling a body that was representative of the people who actually lived in my neighborhood was not the priority. There were two college activists observing, and they expressed interest in organizing around this issue. They seemed to be vaguely connected to the one outspoken middle-aged black woman at the meeting; she was the only other person there who lived on my street. She spoke positively about the condo development and was the only person in the neighborhood I ever met who thought safety could come from more police on our block. I found out later that she supported the proposed condo because her work was in housing development, and she had a lot to gain if the neighborhood increased its economic and social status. Interestingly, all the other (white) homeowners at that meeting were dramatically opposed to the condo development because they lived in mostly fixed-income households that couldn't afford the inevitable increase in their property taxes.

Although most of my neighbors—all the people who I spoke with directly—despised the development plan, and many were already feeling its early effects (increased police violence, landlords encouraged to evict black families in order to rent to white college students, and African business owners kicked out of their buildings), the distant college activists who also organized around gentrification did their work "in the community" at neighborhood meetings like the one I described and at a popular black church on the next block. The college kids and activists from other parts of town kept describing to me that there was no consensus from "the black community" about their position on the development—especially because the minister from that church was initially in favor of it—and so they couldn't organize against the proposed condo; they could only do education about it.

In three years' time, the ground was leveled, the condo was built, and my neighborhood was decimated.

All around me, young white professionals and college kids moved in. My closest friends in the neighborhood were evicted from their home with little warning; the head of their household was the heart of our block. With an open door and delicious food to share, she was a bit of refuge for many of the youths in the neighborhood and knew how to make sure they weren't misbehaving. These friends moved to an apartment in the next city over, and her youngest son was forced to switch schools just after being accepted to join his high school's football team. The landlords of their home did a month of shitty repairs on the house, tripled the rent, and told the college kids who moved in immediately after that the previous tenants had died.

Legitimacy, Justification, Authority

In an attempt to find brown folks to take direction from, white folks often end up tokenizing a specific group whose politics most match their own. "What does the NAACP, Critical Resistance, or the Dream Team think about X?" Or they search out the most visible "leaders" of a community because it is quicker and easier to meet the director of an organization, minister of a church, or politician representing a district than to build real relationships with the people who make up that body. This approach to dismantling racism structurally reinforces the hierarchical power that we're fighting against by asking a small group to represent the views of many people with a variety of different lived experiences. When building an understanding of how to appropriately take leadership from those more affected by oppression, people frequently seek out such a community leader not simply because it's the easiest approach but also because—whether they admit

it or not—they are not just looking to fulfill the need for
guidance; they are seeking out legitimacy, too.

In gaining an anti-oppression education, you learn how you
benefit from the oppression of others because our society values
certain identities. You must come to terms with the fact that you are
granted privilege in our society simply because of what you look
like or where your family comes from—and there is nothing you
can do to fully refuse or redistribute your privilege. The knowledge
of this often comes with a deep sense of white guilt. It can be
paralyzing to know that you are given something that others will
never have, though you have done nothing for it, and have no power
to change this privilege.

This sense of guilt, coupled with the idea that the only ethical
way to act is by taking direction from others, can make one feel
powerless and debased. The model of ally politics puts the burden
of racism exclusively onto white folks as an intentional flipping of
the social hierarchies, while being clear that you can never escape
this iniquity, but offering at least a partial absolution if you can
follow the simple yet narrowly directed penance: *Listen to people of
color. Once you've learned enough from people of color to be a less racist
white person, call out other white people on their racism. You will still
be a racist white person, but you'll be a less racist white person, a more
accountable white person. And at least you can gain the ethical high
ground over other white people so you can tell them what to do.* Time and
time again, we've seen that the salvation model doesn't move us in a
liberatory direction—only toward increased self-righteousness and
plays for power.

To be an ally is to shirk responsibility for your own
actions—legitimizing your position by taking the voice of someone
else, always acting in someone else's name. It's a way of taking

power while simultaneously diminishing your own accountability, because not only are you hiding behind others but you're also obscuring the fact that you're in control of making the choices about who you're listening to—all the while pretending, or convincing yourself, that you're following the leadership of a nonexistent community of people of color or that of the most appropriate black voices. And who are you to decide who the most appropriate anything is? Practically, then, it means finding a black voice who agrees with your position to justify your own desires against the desires of other white people—or mixed-race groups.

Perhaps you've watched or participated in organizing that seeks to *develop the leadership of* individuals who live in a specific neighborhood or work in a particular kind of labor force. This language seems to offer the benevolence of the skills of the organizing group to those who haven't been exposed to such ideas. It is coded language describing a reductive and authoritarian approach to imposing an organizing model on a community of people from the outside. It also conveniently creates spokespeople who can then be used to represent the whole of that (often-heterogeneous) body of people. Over the last several decades, an entire elite class of politicians and spokespeople has been used to politically demobilize the communities they claim to represent.

I frequently hear from antiauthoritarian "white allies" that they are working with authoritarian or nonpartisan community groups, sometimes on projects they don't believe in, because the most important thing is that they follow the leadership of people of color. The unspoken assertion is that there are no antiauthoritarian people of color—or none who are worth working with. Choosing to follow authoritarian people of color in this way invisibilizes all the anarchist or unaligned people of color who would be your comrades in the fight against hierarchical power. Obviously, there is at least as broad a range of political ideologies in communities of color as there are in white communities.

On Sunday, July 14, 2013, in response to the acquittal of Trayvon Martin's killer and the consequenceless murder of black and brown youths in our culture, our small city experienced an uncoordinated collision of a rowdy, angry demonstration and somber, sedentary speak-out. The speak-out was intended to be a space where people could give voice to their sorrow and pain, be held by friends and strangers, and find solace in one another. The marching crowd was lively, vocalizing rage with a bodily frenzy to release.

In the short stretch from the plaza to the courthouse, folks of a variety of ages, races, and genders found rhythm in the streets together, resolute in each others' capacity to rebel on this day of ferocious mourning. The incongruent energies of the two different events met each other abruptly. As the march arrived, small groups tumbled into the speak-out, meeting and chatting with each other. This suddenly overflowing crowd began situating itself, joining the group on the sidewalk and settling into the street in front of it.

The march was clearly an uninvited disruption, and the friend who was holding the space of the speak-out, a prison abolitionist and organizer from a radical African American cultural organization, was encouraging people to quiet down and move on to the sidewalk so the speak-out could continue. Among hesitant attempts to bring the clatter down, the noise of the new crowd slowly started to lower, but rather than giving a little space for a true silence to settle, self-described white allies came to the edge of the sidewalk, physically and verbally corralling people out of the streets and shouting things like, "Shut up! Have some respect! You're all idiots!"

Their comments were pointedly directed to the white folks in the street although the body of people continued to be a mixed-race group. Did this cause uncertainty about how to proceed without clear guidance from a single, united community of color? What do you do according to the white ally handbook when groups of people of color are actively engaged in disagreement? In this case, white allies gave preference to the elder—not coincidentally, the one with the most legitimacy in their radical community.

If these white allies were only trying to diminish their privileged whiteness, I think the respectful thing would have been just to get out of the way.

Perhaps these white allies thought that's what they were doing by addressing their directives solely to the white people in the street. An irritated brigade of bike cops had been tailing the march, however— also nudging folks on to the sidewalk. White allies guilted many demonstrators out of the street, physically attempting to move some people in close proximity to the police, who were trying to do the same thing—without yet putting their hands on anyone.[2] The effect of this was to leave me and another woman of color isolated in the streets with only the police around us because all our comrades had been pushed away.

After listening to many, many speeches—including too many white people taking up too much teary-eyed space—the crowd began to get restless again, though folks didn't want to disrespectfully leave before the speak-out ended. A few of the folks who had marched from the plaza to the speak-out, including several mothers of youths in the nearby jail, rallied the crowd to march to the jail, and the speak-out continued with smaller numbers because most people had either left to go home or had joined the marching crowd, taking the demonstration out into the night.

Did the black folks at the speak-out need a few young white people to speak for them? Certainly none of us needed white radicals to do the police's job for them.

Charity Is to Solidarity, What Ally Is to Affinity

Anarchists and antiauthoritarians clearly differentiate between charity and solidarity—especially thanks to working with indigenous solidarity movements and other international solidarity movements—based on the principles of affinity and mutual aid. Affinity is just what it sounds like: that you can work most easily with people who share your goals, and that your work will be strongest when your relationships are based on trust, friendship, and love. Mutual aid is the idea that we all have a stake in one another's liberation, and that when we can act from that interdependence, we can share with one another as equals.

Charity, however, is something that is given not only because it feels like there is an excess to share but also because it is based in a framework that implies that others inherently *need* the help—that they are unable to take care of themselves and that they would suffer without it. Charity is patronizing and selfish. It establishes some people as *those who assist* and others as *those who need assistance*, stabilizing oppressive paradigms by solidifying people's positions in them.

Autonomy and self-determination are essential to making this distinction as well. Recognizing the autonomy and self-determination of individuals and groups acknowledges their capability. It's an understanding of that group as having something of worth to be gained through interactions with them, whether that thing is a material good or something less tangible, like perspective, joy, or inspiration. The solidarity model dispels the idea of *one* inside and *one* outside, foregrounding how individuals belong to multiple groups and how groups overlap with one another, while simultaneously demanding respect for the identity and self-sufficiency of each of those groups.

The charity and ally models, on the other hand, are so strongly rooted in the ideas of *I* and *the other* that they force people to fit into distinct groups with preordained relationships to one another. According to ally politics, the only way to undermine one's own privilege is to give up one's role as an individual political agent, and follow the lead of those more or differently oppressed. White allies, for instance, are taught explicitly to not seek praise for their ally work—especially from people of color— yet there is often a distinctly self-congratulatory air to the work of allyship, as if the act of their humility is exaggerated to receive the praise they can't ask for. Many white allies do their support work in a way that recentralizes themselves as the only individuals willing to come in and do the hard work of fighting racism for people of color.

Where ally politics suggest that in shifting your role from actor to ally you can diminish your culpability, a liberatory or anarchist approach presumes that each person retains their own agency, insisting that the only way you can be accountable is by acting from your own desires while learning to understand and respond to the desires of other groups. Unraveling our socialized individualization until we can feel how our survival/liberation is infinitely linked to the survival/liberation of others fosters interdependence, as opposed to independence, and enables us to take responsibility for our choices, with no boss or guidance counselor to blame for our decisions.

For a liberating understanding of privilege, each of us must learn our stake in toppling those systems of power to recognize how much we all have to gain in overturning every hierarchy of oppression. For many people, this requires a shift in values. A rights-based discourse around equality would lead us to believe that we could all become atomized middle-class families of any race who are either straight *or* gay married.[3] But anyone who's been on the bottom knows there's never enough room for everyone on the top—or even in the middle.[4] A collective struggle for liberation can offer all of us what we need, but it means seeking things that can be shared in abundance—not those things that are by definition limited resources.

A few years ago, at a May Day march in our town, an unnecessary conflict erupted out of attempts to negotiate within a large crowd about whether or not to march in the street without a permit. At least one group of organized undocumented folks asked others to stay out of the streets because they didn't want to get arrested. In this minimally policed and low-tension situation, rather than beginning conversations about whether it was possible to create space where some people could be in the street and some could be on the sidewalk, several people shifted immediately into control and management mode, increasing the antagonism and artificially creating two opposing sides.

In retrospect, there were numerous ways we could have worked through this respectfully—with better communication both before and during the march. The conflict brought up important questions about how to navigate multiple risk levels within a single event, how to build trust that can translate into plans for safety in the streets, and organizing exit strategies that accommodate different groups of people. But the communication by some people on behalf of others dramatically escalated the situation.

While the march was still in progress, somehow I was tasked with talking to members of a different organization who do work in a nearby neighborhood with many undocumented folks. I approached a group of people who were visibly upset that others remained in the streets, and I had a brief but intense interaction with a man who I'd never met before. I don't remember the exact words that we exchanged, but I remember calmly approaching him and asking him if we could speak about what was going on. He responded by screaming in my face.

After walking away from that interaction, I turned to a woman from the same organization to try again to see if we could strategize some working solutions. She, a graduate student at a nearby private university, launched into a tirade about how I must not understand the disproportionate police harassment that people of color—especially undocumented people—would face if the police chose to attack the march that day. With hard-to-veil irritation, I asked her if she had ever personally experienced police violence or ever spent time in jail. When she answered "no," I told her how ridiculous it felt for her to be making such baseless assumptions about me when I had more stories than I cared to share of police violence in both social and political contexts relating to race and gender. Then I asked her what kind of conversation she expected we could have when she was speaking so stridently about experiences that weren't even hers. She apologized and said that she would just rather talk after the march was over.

After the march, my housemate told me a story from the day that I can only explain as a temporary loss of perspective. While she was walking in the street with her five-year-old nephew, a mutual friend of ours who was frustratedly trying to redirect everyone off the street and on to the sidewalk approached her. With a bullhorn to her mouth, this friend shouted at my housemate to get out of the street. At this point, my housemate said to me with some confusion and sadness, "I thought she was coming to talk to me, but she didn't even say hello to me. She didn't speak my name. She pretended like she didn't know me. I know she knows who I am, but she acted like I was just a body, separated from our hearts."

Community Policing, Power, Authority

Perhaps the least understandable aspect of ally politics to me is the overwhelming tendency for people, who otherwise seem to aspire to relationships free of domination, to try to exert control over others. Is it because when we feel like we occupy the most legitimate or objectively most justified position (often according to a strangely quantitative evaluation of those who are most wronged by social oppressions), it is easy to inflate our sense of righteousness? Or is it that when we feel like we have the most information—or most connections to other "important" groups—we can make decisions for others better than they can make for themselves?

Respecting individual and group autonomy means that we don't need a bunch of fucking managers; it means that no matter how well positioned or knowledgeable you are, people can communicate and resolve conflicts best when speaking from their direct experiences and with genuine humility. Some of the first skills taught in conflict resolution, facilitation, and de-escalation trainings are how not to speak for others; you learn that you break trust when trying to represent others without their consent.

During the antiglobalization years at the turn of the twenty-first century, I frequently found myself in baffling arguments about the use of "violence" in demonstrations with pacifists or others who self-described as adhering to a strict code of nonviolence. Many of the same folks who argued that we shouldn't do anything that could hurt someone else's property consistently yelled at their companions until they felt threatened, and engaged in intensely damaging emotional manipulations and passive-aggressive maneuvers in meetings and during demonstrations. Countless times, I saw "nonviolent" demonstrators physically hurt other protesters by attempting to drag them out of the streets for spray painting a wall or breaking a window.

Why do people feel justified in trying to pacify others—often with little context for one another? Such vehement attempts to try to contain other's rage and rebellion leads to an unnecessary escalation of conflict between those of us who should be able to struggle together instead of against one another.

We're Not Trying to Get Comfortable; We're Trying to Get Free

We are told that resistance lies in "speaking truth to power" rather than attacking power materially. We are told by an array of highly trained "white allies" that the very things we need to do in order to free ourselves from domination cannot be done by us because we're simply too vulnerable to state repression. At mass rallies, we're replayed endless empty calls for revolution and militancy from a bygone era while in practice being forced to fetishize our spiritual powerlessness.

—Escalating Identity, "Who Is Oakland?"

Revolutionary struggle is indeed *radically unsafe*. It is a lifelong aspiration that can and does mean prison or death for some of us, and an awareness that these risks can intensify based on the different parts of our identities is necessary. Yet the concept and role of ally politics has mutated this awareness into a practice of collective policing by would-be managers who are shielded from criticism by the authority of a depersonalized, stereotyped other.

The ally framework individualizes structures of oppression, constantly shifting action away from attacking those structures to an emphasis instead on individual behaviors. The focus on individual privilege has become such a popular political discourse precisely because it often leaves unquestioned the very structures that create that privilege. Though it is necessary to understand how we are shaped by systematic forms of oppression, if we aim to collectively dismantle the structures of domination that enable these privileges to exist, the individual transformations must happen concurrently.

The ally framework also obscures the fact that there is no single community of color for white people to ally themselves to; rather, there is a heterogeneous mass of overlapping and conflicting individuals and groups. The crisis of representation this creates frequently results in well-intentioned allies stealing agency away from people of color who disagree with the established, institutionalized groups being exalted—only reinforcing hierarchies of legitimacy and policing the boundaries of political approach by throwing the weight of their privileges behind those who already have more power.

We all experience fear and doubt, or are unsure how to proceed at times, but we must hold those fears as our own, as we must hold our desires for freedom as our own. When we act on behalf of an imagined "other," it makes genuine communication around tactics, strategy, and solidarity impossible, shattering our relationships and fueling mistrust where there could be affinity.

Our relationships are not what we need to be breaking.

The typical counter-rioter, who risked injury and arrest to walk the streets urging rioters to "cool it," was an active supporter of existing social institutions. He was, for example, far more likely than either the rioter or the noninvolved to feel that this country is worth defending in a major war. His actions and his attitudes reflected his substantially greater stake in the social system; he was considerably better educated and more affluent than either the rioter or the noninvolved.

—US Riot Commission Report, 1968

A Critique of Ally Politics

Just because You Feel Like You're the One Who Broke It, Doesn't Mean You Need to Fix It

Growing up in this culture, we're taught so much hatred for the parts of ourselves as well as others who are different from the mainstream or dominant culture. We learn what it means to have good hair or a good nose; we're told our lightest-skinned sibling is the most beautiful; we're taught shame about the size and shape of our bodies, about who and what we desire.

White supremacy, misogyny, and all the ideologies that create "the other" are at once superficial and incredibly rooted within us.

It is inevitable that as we develop a critical analysis of the various axes of identity—race, gender, class, ability, and more—we will experience deeply personal and political moments of self-realization—about ourselves and our relationships with others as well as about the way this culture functions. It is important and positive that we make those kinds of developments in identifying how oppression works, internally and externally. Yet we must not get so caught up in our own self-discoveries that we unthinkingly put the emotional weight of those breakthrough moments on others who live daily with the realities we are just beginning to understand.

Trayvon Martin became a symbol for this generation of the normalcy of violence perpetrated against criminalized, black bodies. The events around his death and his murderer's acquittal were dramatically emotional for many of my younger white friends; it was clearly a moment of realization about something big. In conversations with other friends of color, however, the pain of the unexceptionality of this case was always at the forefront. We all know this is standard treatment for youths of color. A young friend of mine put it best when he said, "Of course I'm mad; I'm always mad at the police. But I don't know why anyone is surprised. This is how we're always treated. I just wish those white girls would stop crying and get up."

Here are a few tips.

Slow down: Don't try to fix it. Don't rush to find an answer or act out of your guilt. Remember that many of your comrades have been doing this work for a long time and experience the kind of oppression you're learning about more acutely than you. It didn't start with you and isn't going to end with you.

Keep it internal: Don't take up too much space with your thoughts and emotions. Be sensitive to the fact that folks are in a variety of places in relation to what you're working through; don't force conversations on others, especially through the guise of public organizing.

Write about it: Give yourself the unedited space to feel all the things you need to, but know that it may hurt others if you share your feelings unthinkingly.

Read about it: Look for resources from people of a variety of political ideologies and experiences of identity to challenge yourself and get the widest range of input.

Listen to older people: Listening to stories from your eighty-year-old African American neighbor when you're working through questions around racism will likely be thought provoking, regardless of their political ideology or your life experience. Don't underestimate what a little perspective can do for you.

Don't make your process the problem of your comrades: Be careful not to centralize yourself, your stake in fixing the problem, or your ego. Work it out on your own and with close friends and mentors.

Notes

1   This extract and the following ones in this piece are experiential stories from the author.

2   Never put your hands on anyone in front of the police—especially people you understand to be even vaguely on your side. This only increases the likelihood that the police will escalate to using physical force.

3   This sounds like the dream of the mainstream civil rights movement: black and brown politicians equally in control of the military, police, and prisons; or the dream of the mainstream feminist movement: lipstick and respect in the boardroom. Goals like these have always kept anarchists on the fringes of mainstream rights-based movements pushing for a more holistic analysis that inevitably necessitates more radical action.

4   For every Scandinavia, there must be an Africa—even if there are parts of Africa in Scandinavia and vice versa.

Accomplices

Not
Allies

Accomplices Not Allies:
Abolishing the Ally Industrial Complex

The attribution on the original zine version of this piece reads "an Indigenous perspective." It was written and published by **Indigenous Action Media**, www.indigenousaction.org.

This provocation is intended to intervene in some of the current tensions around solidarity and support work as the current trajectories are counterliberatory from our perspective. Special thanks goes to DS in Phoenix for convos that lead to this zine, and all those who provided comments, questions, and disagreements. Don't construe this as being for "white, young, middle-class allies," just for paid activists, nonprofits, or as a friend said, "downwardly mobile anarchists or students." There are many so-called allies in the migrant rights struggle who support "comprehensive immigration reform," which involves the further militarization of indigenous lands.

The ally industrial complex has been established by activists whose careers depend on the "issues" they work to address. These nonprofit capitalists advance their careers off the struggles they ostensibly support. They often work in the guise of "grassroots" or "community based," and are not necessarily tied to any organization.

They build organizational or individual capacity and power, establishing themselves comfortably among the top ranks in their hierarchy of oppression as they strive to become the ally "champions" of the most oppressed. While the exploitation of solidarity and support is nothing new, the commodification and exploitation of allyship is a growing trend in the activism industry.

Anyone who concerns themselves with anti-oppression struggles and collective liberation has at some point either participated in workshops, read zines, or been part of deep discussions on how to be a "good" ally. You can now pay hundreds of dollars to go to esoteric institutes for an allyship certificate in anti-oppression. You can go through workshops and receive an allyship badge. In order to commodify struggle, it must first be objectified. This is exhibited in how "issues" are "framed" and "branded." Where struggle is commodity, allyship is currency.

Ally has also become an identity, disembodied from any real mutual understanding of support. The term "ally" has been rendered ineffective and meaningless.

Accomplices Not Allies

ac·com·plice
noun: accomplice; plural noun: accomplices
a person who helps another commit a crime.

There exists a fiercely unrelenting desire to achieve total liberation, with the land and together.

At some point there is a "we," and we most likely will have to work together. This means, at the least, formulating mutual understandings that are not entirely antagonistic; otherwise, we may find ourselves, our desires, and our struggles to be incompatible.

There are certain understandings that may not be negotiable. There are contradictions that we must come to terms with, and certainly we will do this on our own terms.

But we need to know who has our backs, or more appropriately: Who is with us at our sides?

The risks of an ally who provides support or solidarity (usually on a temporary basis) in a fight are much different than that of an accomplice. When we fight back or forward, together, becoming complicit in a struggle toward liberation, we are accomplices. Abolishing allyship can occur through the criminalization of support and solidarity.

While the strategies and tactics of asserting (or abolishing, depending on your view) social and political power may be diverse, there are some hard lessons that it would be best not to forget.

Consider the following to be a guide for identifying points of intervention against the ally industrial complex.

"Salvation aka Missionary Work and Self-Therapy"

Allies all too often carry romantic notions of oppressed folks they wish to "help." These are the ally "saviors" who see victims and tokens instead of people.

This victimization becomes a fetish for the worst of the allies in forms of exotification, manarchism, 'splaining, POC sexploitation, and so on. This kind of relationship generally fosters exploitation between both the oppressed and oppressor. The ally and allied-with become entangled in an abusive relationship. Generally neither can see it until it's too late. This relationship can also digress into codependency, which means they have robbed each other of their own power. Ally "saviors" have a tendency to create dependency on them and their function as support. No one is here to be saved; we don't need "missionary allies" or pity.

Guilt is also a primary ally motivating factor. Even if never admitted, guilt and shame generally function as motivators in the consciousness of an oppressor who realizes that they are operating on the wrong side. While guilt and shame are powerful emotions, think about what you're doing before you make another community's struggle into your therapy session. Of course, acts of resistance and liberation can be healing, but tackling guilt, shame, and other trauma requires a much different focus, or at least an explicit and consensual focus. What kinds of relationships are built on guilt and shame?

"Exploitation and Co-optation"

Those who co-opt are only there to advance self-interests (usually it's either notoriety or financial). As these "allies" seek to impose their agenda, they out themselves. The "radical," more-militant-than-thou "grassroots" organizers are keen on seeking out "sexy" issues to co-opt (for notoriety, ego, super ally, or most radical ally), and they set the terms of engagement or dictate what struggles get amplified or marginalized regardless of whose homelands they're operating on. The nonprofit establishment or nonprofit-industrial complex also seeks out "sexy" or "fundable" issues to co-opt and exploit, as these are ripe for the grant funding that they covet.

Too often, indigenous liberation struggles for life and land, by nature, directly confront the entire framework on which this colonial and capitalist society is based. This is threatening to potential capitalist funders, so some groups are forced to compromise radical or liberatory work for funding, and others become alienated and further invisibilized or subordinated to tokenism. Co-opters most often show up to the fight when the battle has already escalated and it's a little too late.

These entities almost always propose trainings, workshops, and action camps, and offer other specialized expertise in acts of patronization. These folks are generally paid huge salaries for their "professional" activism, get overinflated grants for logistics and "organizational capacity building," and struggles may become further exploited as "poster struggles" for their funders.

Additionally, these skills most likely already exist within the communities or they are tendencies that need only be provoked into action.

These aren't just dynamics practiced by large so-called nongovernmental organizations; individuals are adept at this self-serving tactic as well.

Co-optation also functions as a form of liberalism. Allyship can perpetuate a neutralizing dynamic by co-opting original liberatory intent into a reformist agenda.

Certain folks in the struggles (usually movement "personalities") who don't upset the ally establishment status quo can be rewarded with inclusion in the ally industry.

"Self-Proclaiming / Confessional Allies"

All too often folks show up with an "I am here to support you!" attitude that they wear like a badge, ultimately making struggles out to feel like an extracurricular activity that they are getting "ally points" for. Self-professed allies may even have anti-oppression principles and values as window dressing. Perhaps you've seen this quote by Lilla Watson on their materials: "If you come here to help me, you're wasting your time. If you come because your liberation is bound up with mine, then let us work together." They are keen to posture, but their actions are inconsistent with their assertions.

Meaningful alliances aren't imposed; they are consented on. The self-proclaimed allies have no intention to abolish the entitlement that compelled them to impose their relationship on those they claim to ally with.

"Parachuters"

Parachuters rush to the front lines seemingly from out of nowhere. They literally move from one hot or sexy spot to the next. They also fall under the "savior" and "self-proclaimed" categories as they mostly come from specialized institutes, organizations, and think tanks. They've been through the trainings, workshops, lectures, and so on; they are the "experts" so they know "what is best." This paternalistic attitude is implicit in the structures (nonprofits, institutes, etc.) that these "allies" derive their awareness of the "issues" from. Even if they reject their own nonprofit programming, they are ultimately reactionary, entitled, and patronizing, or positioning with power-over those they proclaim allyship with. It's structural patronization that is rooted in the same dominion of heteropatriarchal white supremacy.

Parachuters are usually missionaries with more funding.

"Academics and Intellectuals"

Although sometimes directly from communities in struggle, intellectuals and academics also fit neatly in all these categories.

Their role in struggle can be extremely patronizing. In many cases, the academic maintains institutional power above the knowledge and skill base of the community/ies in struggle. Intellectuals are most often fixated on unlearning oppression. This lot generally doesn't have its feet on the ground, but is quick to be critical of those who do. Should we desire to merely "unlearn" oppression, or smash it to fucking pieces and have its very existence gone?

An accomplice as academic would seek ways to leverage resources and material support and/or betray their institution to further liberation struggles. An intellectual accomplice would strategize with, not for, and not be afraid to pick up a hammer.

"Gatekeepers"

Gatekeepers seek power over, not with, others. They are known for the tactics of controlling and/or withholding information, resources, connections, support, and so forth. Gatekeepers come from the outside and within. When exposed, they are usually rendered ineffective (so long as there are effective accountability and responsibility mechanisms).

Gatekeeping individuals and organizations, like "savior allies," also have a tendency to create dependency on them and their function as support. They have a tendency to dominate or control.

"Navigators and Floaters"

The "navigating" ally is someone who is familiar with or skilled in jargon, and maneuvers through spaces or struggles, yet doesn't have meaningful dialogue (by avoiding debates or remaining silent) or take meaningful action beyond their personal comfort zones (this exists with entire organizations too). They uphold their power and, by extension, the dominant power structures by not directly attacking them.

"Ally" here is more clearly defined as the act of making personal projects out of other folks' oppression. These are lifestyle allies, who act like passively participating or simply using the right terminology is support. When shit goes down, they are the first to bail. They don't stick around to take responsibility for their behavior. When confronted, they often blame others, and attempt to dismiss or delegitimize concerns.

Accomplices aren't afraid to engage in uncomfortable, unsettling, and/or challenging debates or discussions.

Floaters are "allies" that hop from group to group and issue to issue, never being committed enough, but always wanting their presence felt and their voices heard. They tend to disappear when it comes down to being held accountable or taking responsibility for fucked-up behavior.

Floaters are folks you can trust to tell the cops to "fuck off" but never engage in mutual risk, constantly put others at risk, are quick to be authoritarian about other peoples' overstepping privileges, but never check their own. They basically are action-junkie tourists who never want to be part of paying the price, planning, or responsibility, but always want to be held up as worthy of being respected for "having been there" when a rock needed throwing, bloc needed forming, and so on.

This dynamic is also important to be aware of for threats of infiltration. Provocateurs are notorious floaters going from place to place, never being accountable to their words or actions. Infiltration doesn't necessarily have to come from the state; the same impacts can occur by "well-meaning" allies. It's important to note that calling out infiltrators bears serious implications and shouldn't be attempted without concrete evidence.

"Acts of Resignation"

Resignation of agency is a by-product of the allyship establishment. At first the dynamic may not seem problematic. After all, why would it be an issue with those who benefit from systems of oppression to reject or distance themselves from those benefits and behaviors (like entitlement, etc.) that accompany them? In the worst cases, "allies" themselves act paralyzed, believing it's their duty as a "good ally." There is a difference between acting for others, with others, and for one's own interests. Be explicit.

You wouldn't find an accomplice resigning their agency or capabilities as an act of "support." They would find creative ways to weaponize their privilege (or more clearly, their rewards of being part of an oppressor class) as an expression of social war. Otherwise, we end up with a bunch of anticiv/primitivist appropriators or anarcho-hipsters, when saboteurs would be preferred.

Suggestions for Some Ways Forward
for Anticolonial Accomplices

Allyship is the corruption of radical spirit and imagination; it's the dead end of decolonization. The ally establishment co-opts decolonization as a banner to fly at its unending anti-oppression gala. What is not understood is that decolonization is a threat to the very existence of settler "allies." No matter how liberated you are, if you are still occupying indigenous lands, you are still a colonizer.

Decolonization (the process of restoring indigenous identity) can be very personal and should be differentiated, though not disconnected, from anticolonial struggle.

The work of an accomplice in anticolonial struggle is to attack colonial structures and ideas.

The starting point is to articulate your relationship to indigenous peoples whose lands you are occupying. This is beyond acknowledgment or recognition. This can be particularly challenging for "nonfederally recognized" indigenous peoples as they are invisiblized by the state and the invaders occupying their homelands.

It may take time to establish lines of communication, especially as some folks may have already been burned by outsiders. If you do not know where or how to contact folks, do some groundwork and research (but don't rely on anthropological sources; they are Eurocentric), and pay attention. Try to do more listening than speaking and planning.

In long-term struggles, communication may be ruptured between various factions; there are no easy ways to address this. Don't try to work the situation out, but communicate openly with consideration of the points below.

Sometimes other indigenous peoples are "guests" on others' homelands yet are tokenized as the indigenous representatives for the "local struggles." This dynamic also perpetuates settler colonialism. A lot of people also assume indigenous folks are all on the same page "politically"; we're definitely not.

While there may be times folks have the capacity and patience to do so, be aware of the dynamics perpetuated by hand-holding.

Understand that it is not our responsibility to hold your hand through a process to be an accomplice.

Accomplices listen with respect for the range of cultural practices and dynamics that exist within various indigenous communities.

Accomplices aren't motivated by personal guilt or shame; they may have their own agenda, but they are explicit.

Accomplices are realized through mutual consent and build trust. They don't just have our backs; they are at our side, or in their own spaces confronting and unsettling colonialism. *As accomplices, we are compelled to become accountable and responsible to each other; that is the nature of trust.*

Don't wait around for anyone to proclaim you to be an accomplice; you certainly cannot proclaim it yourself. You just are or you are not. The lines of oppression are already drawn.

Direct action is really the best and may be the only way to learn what it is to be an accomplice. We're in a fight, so be ready for confrontation and consequence.

If You Are Wondering Whether to Get Involved with or Support an Organization

Be suspect of anyone and any organization who professes allyship, decolonization work, and/or wears their relationships with indigenous peoples as a badge.

Use some of the points above to determine primary motives.

Look at the organization's funding. Who is getting paid? How are they transparent? Who's defining the terms? Who sets the agenda? Do campaigns align with what the needs are on the ground?

Are there local, grassroots indigenous people directly involved with the decision making?

Coconspirators

Coconspirators

This is an excerpt from a recent interview in *Mask* magazine
with **Neal Shirley** and **Saralee Stafford**, coauthors of
*Dixie Be Damned: 300 Years of Insurrection in the American
South* (AK Press).

Question: [Your] book covers many cases of cross-racial
alliances, and the various ways that poor and rebellious white
people were made invisible or erased from accounts about
uprisings. You go on to talk about how race was constructed as a
way to paint rebellion as a threat against all white people, thereby
misrepresenting the interest that poor white people had in the
success of rebellions and in participating in them. How does this
observation inform how you think about race, identity, and
revolt today?

Answer: Let's start with the "outside agitator" as a white
northerner, anarchist or communist, before we get to the question
of erasing rebellious white subjects. From the early days of chattel
slavery up until today, the outside agitator theory supports the white
supremacist narrative that black and brown people are too ignorant
or lazy to rebel on their own. Even in the distinctly black rebellion
in 1868 in Ogeechee, Georgia, where the battle cry was "No white
man should live between the two Ogeechee [rivers]," plantation
owners were trying to say it was radical labor activists from up
north in collusion with the governor who started these rebellions.

We have seen the various ways that the white, outside agitator myth was used by the police and their media spokespeople to inflame internal conflicts and delegitimize black, armed rebellion from Ferguson to Baltimore in the last year. It's not only absurd; it's racist and directly reifies the colonial notion that black people were providentially ordained into slavery. When you do this research and really break down what's going on when people employ these narratives, you realize that this isn't just propaganda to disparage armed self-defense, arson, and riots. It also strives to create the notion that all white people in these revolts either are cops, infiltrators, or outsiders who have no genuine reason to be angry. That then makes developing any kind of actual affinity on the ground—even if it's just some practical shit like washing someone's eyes from teargas—all the more difficult.

So on the one hand, you have the white participant in revolt as that of both an outsider and agitator, which reaffirms the idea that white people and people of color are all somehow completely removed from each other's day-to-day lives, and that when revolts happen, white folks only show up to stir up these normally peaceful, unmoved black people. On the other hand, you have the disappearance of white folks from certain uprisings because to imagine them as coconspirators would destabilize white supremacy. These people have often been called "race traitors" or "white trash," or have actually been rewritten as black or brown by the media/state to erase the evidence that there has been cross-racial, class-based, and regional-based solidarity from the first day that the ships arrived in Jamestown to a few weeks ago in Baltimore.

The other problem, however, is that a lot of white people today want credit for being good "allies" in these rebellions. A lot of times we get involved in shit and we start to make it about class instead of race, or about how we're all against the police and don't really want to talk about the systematic terror, torture, and genocide of black people. At other times we use obscure, romantic language about destroying various totalities: society, identity, the existent, civilization, the list goes on, … and we mean that to include white supremacy as a systematic force of organizing society, but frequently that gets lost in our propaganda and we sound like poets who don't want to be asked what we mean.

The way we as authors tend to look at identity is based on something that is forged in resistance and rejection, which is perhaps different than how most people talk about identity as some kind of positive and emancipatory category. Anarchist Panther Ashanti Alston once said in a speech, "I think of being black not so much as an ethnic category but as an oppositional force or touchstone for looking at situations differently." For instance, we see blackness emerge not only as a state of not being white, as a differentiation, marking of otherness, or marking of bondage. It also evolves as an identity in resistance to whiteness, capital, and enslavement. To be black was often to refuse and attack those systems. Perhaps paradoxically, this became an identity that could then be placed onto nonblack subjects who were also resisting those systems, though that happened only superficially. For example, multiracial subjects who were frequently written about as white when not rebelling became "mulattoes" during rebellions. The formerly European maroons in the Great Dismal Swamp, for instance, were sometimes called "tawny" by the media and even fought in black regiments during the US Civil War.

And what does this tell us about whiteness? It definitely shows there's a crisis of legitimacy and authenticity there. But what it also points to is that when white people decide to not remain complicit with white supremacist social life and do things that attack that construction of power, their own identity as "white" comes into question. Of course, the difference being that all white folks have to do to fold right back into the safety and legitimacy that our whiteness gives us is to stop actively participating in struggles.

Perhaps there is a messianic moment that delivers us from identity during the insurrection or whatever. But the idea that being in the streets together or living in a commune can dissolve the identities that divide and individualize us is perhaps a temporal reality—one that functions as mythology when we're actually back at work, on the subway, or in school. There's a tension there that we all continue to wrestle with. For as long as these structures exist, we can't just excuse ourselves from asking critical questions about identity, race, and affinity, and that in turn forces us to think about the kinds of relationships we build in between these swells of conflict and activity.

Outside

Agitators

Outside Agitators

This fragment of a longer piece by **J. B.** was taken from "You Can't Shoot Us All," published in 2010 as a pamphlet-size memoir of the Oscar Grant movement in Oakland.

When the South has trouble with its Negroes—when the Negroes refuse to remain in their "place"—it blames "outside agitators."

—James Baldwin

The term "outside agitator" was popularized during the civil rights struggles of the 1950s, when southern politicians would blame the growing unrest in exploited black communities on the presence of (often-white) radicals from outside the city. Presently, it is a term used by Oakland politicians (and aspiring politicians) to try to keep the situation under control, to prevent local marginalized people from realizing the power they have.

Today, we face enemies that we could have never conceived of before this. Sometimes, it's the people who pretend to be on your side who are the most dangerous enemies. The nonprofit world has, for eighteen months, waged a campaign against this movement.

Many nonprofits that function independently of the local government have disparaged us. They oppose collective uprisings and spontaneous activity because they feel the need to control the movement. These organizations view themselves as the saviors of the downtrodden; when dominated people rise up on their own terms, it threatens the position of leadership that these organizations occupy in their imaginary worlds.

We have also come under attack from nonprofits that operate entirely under the influence of the city government. One of these city-funded nonprofits has taken up a full-fledged assault against us, using some of the $2 million in city money it has received to wage a propaganda campaign against the unity that we have found with each other through this struggle. This nonprofit has even used city money to pay young people to come to its indoctrination workshops, where the organization speaks of the evils of people coming together and standing up to their enemies.

It has also helped to spread the absurd logic of the mayor's office that only people born and raised in Oakland have the right to take to the streets. This micronationalism is an attempt to foster collaboration between disenfranchised people and their exploiters in a united front against the enigmatic "outsiders."

It is incorrect to assert that nonprofits of this type have motivations of their own. They are simply the hip mouthpieces of the city government that funds them. Their agenda is the agenda of the mayor's office and police department. They use the language of "peace" to try to preserve the institutions that created them. We have never been concerned with their peace. The peace of the powerful is the silent war waged against the dispossessed.

In the past, our enemies have attempted to divide movements by distinguishing the "good" element from the "destructive" element. This time, it seems that the primary division they created was not between the "peaceful" and "violent" but instead a racial division wedged between groups in the uncontrollable element in an attempt to neutralize our collective strength.

I, identifying with a man whose photograph was not unlike my own reflection, wondered if people who did not see themselves in Oscar Grant at least saw in his image their friend, their neighbor, their classmate, someone whose life was worth fighting over. I hoped that there were white people who, after watching a video of a black man being murdered by the police, would be angry enough to break windows. In time, I met these people, because they fought alongside us, throwing bottles and chunks of concrete, cursing the police and writing the names of the dead on the walls of this city. 105

Outside Agitators

We Are All
Oscar Grant

(?)

We Are All Oscar Grant(?): Attacking White Supremacy in the Rebellions and Beyond

This essay by **Finn Feinberg** is from the revised edition in 2012 of the zine-style compilation titled *Unfinished Acts: January Rebellions, Oakland, California, 2009.*

The project of sustained insurrectionary activity must constantly chip away at the foundations of white supremacy. Although anarchist practice is assumed to be inherently antiracist, evidence of this is often hard to find. This should be obvious, but it is worth repeating: to loathe the United States of America and capitalism, to want them destroyed, means the task set in front of us is to attack and abolish the racial order that has enabled these beasts.

The Oscar Grant rebellions give us a little glimpse of people in the Bay Area doing just that. In the riots, we saw the collective power of black and brown young people battling, with little fear, against the established white supremacist order. Surprisingly, there also was a small showing of white people in the rebellion as well. This brief show of solidarity from white folks—both those who do have experiences of being criminalized, poor young people and those who do not—reveals that white folks can have agency to violently oppose a clearly white supremacist institution side by side with nonwhites without pretending to share identity or experience where it is not the case. Also, contrary to dominant narratives that paint the essence of riots as male-dominated affairs, many queer and female (mostly nonwhite) comrades took their place at the front lines, participating in the supposedly masculine rebellion without apprehension. Their participation is significant as it throws a wrench into the logic of peace-loving, docile femininity and what self-determination looks like for some who live on the axis of gender tyranny and white supremacy. Although most police shooting victims are black and brown men, the Oscar Grant rebellions show us that their deaths affect and outrage masses of people across race and gender lines.

During each demonstration and riot where folks gathered to express their rage in the face of Oscar Grant's murder and what his death represented, the chant "We are all Oscar Grant!" rang through the downtown streets of Oakland. For those indoctrinated into the logic popularized by nonprofit organizing culture that treats identity and experiences of oppression as one and the same, it is inappropriate for anyone other than people of color to yell this slogan. This critique falls flat for many as it assumes that we yell this to declare collective victimhood rather than a collective proclamation to not be victims.

For those of us who are poor and black or brown, anarchist or not, we cannot claim to share every experience with Oscar Grant, but we do live our days with the knowledge that we could have the same fate as him if our class society, with its racialized implications, is not reckoned with. For women and queers, especially those of us who also are not white, our experiences may not mirror Oscar Grant's life and death, but we too live with the sick threat of violence on our bodies by both the patriarchal, trans misogynist, and racist state, and the individuals who replicate the attitudes and oppressive actions of the state. For any of us who are not poor and black or brown, anarchist or not, we may not usually fear for our lives when police are near, but it is plain as day that if we don't all start acting like it's our very lives at stake as well, not only are we an accessory to these racist deaths, we foolishly assume we will not be next. For whites who joined in this chorus of "We are all Oscar Grant!" this declaration meant that we refused to be another white person, if being white means letting this shit continue to slide for the bogus justification that this racist violence keeps society (read: white people) safe.

The spirit behind "We are all Oscar Grant!" is indicative of the attitude of the Oscar Grant rebellion as a whole. Despite the fact that many of us did not generally know each other before those nights because of the racial divisions imposed by society and maintained by ourselves, we found glorious moments of struggling with one another in the streets where our identities or experiences were not collapsed into a faux sameness.

Toward a Never-Ending Uprising

Moments of cross-racial solidarity and the crumbling of various social barriers were particularly evident on these few, warm rebellious nights in January 2009. This should not lead one to believe that the days between or beyond these riotous evenings were days where police shootings ended, or where social distinctions and hierarchies disappeared, or solidarity was a given. Disappointingly, we all went back to our usual lives as individuals: dodging cops, reading about horrendous police brutality on Facebook, struggling to make ends meet, drinking too much, dragging ourselves to school, or doing our hustles. Whatever different "normal" is for each person who ran wild in the streets of Oakland in the name of Oscar Grant, we went back to it.

For some, "normalcy" is going to jail.

Throughout the Oscar Grant and then Occupy movements, despite whatever demographics took part in the street festivities, it has remained that those stuck with heavy sentences have been black and/or homeless, many of whom were on probation or parole. This fact should not reinforce the myth that only black and brown youths were arrested but should instead highlight the intensely racist nature of the judicial system. If we are to struggle alongside these folks in moments of uproar, we must recognize that they often have higher stakes if they get caught up in the bullshit justice system. When folks already criminalized by the system put themselves on the line, there should be unrelenting pressure on the system to the scale that we know we are capable of with hundreds of anarchists in the Bay. It's not that black and brown rebels are people to feel sorry for and "help," nor feel protective of and "keep safe" as they rage in the streets, as paternalistic leftists might suggest. But if we take seriously that these fellow rioters will be our comrades and coconspirators for bigger and badder insurrections to come, we cannot let them hang out to dry when they're going down for the same acts that we (allegedly) took part in.

Do some of us—whites and people of all races—find ourselves shrugging and accepting that it is normal for black people to go to jail? We feel indignant when someone is murdered by the state, but somehow feel less moved when someone is kidnapped and held captive by the state. Why is it so shocking to us when a white anarchist comrade goes down for a year, but not when many black or homeless comrades are locked up repeatedly, and for longer sentences?

There is an unquestioned and deep-seated logic embedded in the psyche of US society that has taught all of us, white or not, and anarchist or not, that white bodies are to be cared for and coddled, while nonwhite and especially black bodies are assumed to be criminal, expendable, and not to be trusted. Without consciously and intentionally bucking against this logic, black deaths—be they psychological, physical, slow, or fast—will remain the norm, and will make any attempt at insurrectionary or revolutionary activity smack of insincerity and history lessons unlearned.[1]

It's more obvious than ever that leftist politicians and NGO admins with grant-money dollar signs in their eyes have done and will do little to address everyday problems for—or with—folks from Oakland's hoods. The question that anarchists must seriously grapple with is, Do we blow just as much hot air as our leftist enemies?

Beyond our lackluster efforts in countering the state repression of our fellow rebels, have we also left the response to everyday atrocities to be tackled by those who we know are invested in the very institutions that perpetuate these everyday oppressions and exploitation? It's fine (great even) that we can't stand to do reformist campaigns to make daily life more tolerable. That being the case, what are we willing to do? If we can't stand the victim-making rhetoric that strips power from the very people who must wield it, if we loathe representational politics and neither want to speak for or do anything for anyone who is "not us," where does this leave us? For many of us who are white and/or male anarchists, we know that calls to "check privilege" and tiptoe around language do little to nothing to topple racial and gender hierarchies. Throwing ourselves into the role of social service providers also misses the boat. What strategies are left available? Are these theoretical dead ends that cannot be solved, or are we lacking the resolve and imagination necessary to answer these questions through meaningful deeds. Given the fact that we found ourselves struggling around the atrocious murder of Oscar Grant, why don't we see ourselves in similar ruptures sparked by the daily abuses faced by oppressed people, our neighbors, our kids' friends, and our coworkers?

It's Going Down with or without Us

Insurrections, rioting, mass expropriations, occupations, and all sorts of unimaginable forms of class warfare are not only inevitable but also are taking place all over with more frequency and veraciousness as the crisis that is capitalism deepens.

It is crystal clear that the deprived, exploited, and violated have organized, and will continue to do so, formally and informally, to the demise of their oppressors, those who remain neutral, or each other.

The side of history on which we find ourselves is not determined by whether or not we share the experiences of one horror or another, or how we individually identify, but instead on our own resolution to see the end of each of these miseries that perpetuate this racist, capitalist, shit show called society.

To those of us who cooperatively destroyed capitalist and state property, humiliated and terrified police and yuppies, and found power and a sense of dignity together that we had never known before, and to those of us who found ourselves high off the lack of social divisions in the streets of Oakland during a moment of open revolt, let's figure out ways to maintain these moments outside a riot. We must play a part in continuing this rebellious trajectory as a motley crew of insurrectionists or be deemed irrelevant—or worse, the recipients of the wrath of the "righteous people who anger slowly, but rage undammed."[2]

Notes

[1]   It is worth noting that whiteness as a social category was created and promoted by plantation owners and other capitalists in the early days of America's colonization in order to put a wedge between the workers they were exploiting. Before this, poor, fair-skinned people were dirty Irish, criminals expelled from England, indentured servants, trash, and so on. This was done through both extreme terror campaigns against those who coconspired in insurrections on plantations, shipping docks, and urban centers as well as by convincing the poor, recently named "whites" that they had special privileges that were under threat by those of darker skin color, thus creating a perfect situation for the no-longer-shook capitalists when whites began putting racial solidarity above class solidarity. So nowadays, most persons of color live in crippling poverty while white capitalists still are rich fucks ruling over them. What is often overlooked, however, is that in exchange for accepting the privileged position of white, whites still make up half of those in the United States living in poverty, left to the whims of the same ruthless whites in power. That is to say, selling out one's class members and helping to prop up a racist system through clutching on to a psychology that our white friends, family, and selves are somehow more exalted than nonwhite folks has for hundreds of years effectively been a shot into our own feet.

[2]   "This monster—the monster they've engendered in me—will return to torment its maker, from the grave, the pit, the profoundest pit. Hurl me into the next existence, the descent into hell won't turn me. I'll crawl back to dog his trail forever. They won't defeat my revenge, never, never. I'm part of a righteous people who anger slowly, but rage undammed. We'll gather at his door in such a number that the rumbling of our feet will make the earth tremble" (George Jackson, Blood in My Eye, 1970).

Not
Murdered

and
Not

Missing

Not Murdered and Not Missing: Rebelling against Colonial Gender Violence

This piece by **Leanne Simpson** appeared on March 15, 2014, on Nations Rising, http://nationsrising.org, with thanks to Miigwech/Nia:wen/Mahsi Cho, Tara Williamson, Melody McKiver, Jessica Danforth, Glen Coulthard, and Jarrett Martineau for editing previous drafts.

I've learned a tremendous amount over the past months from Loretta Saunders, Bella Laboucan-McLean, and all the other indigenous people who we've had violently ripped away from us in this last little while. Part of me feels shaky to admit this, because intellectually, and even personally, I know or am supposed to know a lot about gender violence. But there are things I don't say in public. There are things I think that I am not brave enough to say because of the pain of not being heard, of being betrayed, and appearing weak to my indigenous friends or colleagues is too much to bear. There are places I only go with other indigenous comrades who I trust intimately.

That ends here.

It ends here for Loretta, Bella, and all the other brilliant minds and fierce hearts we've lost. It ends here.

This is my rebellion. This is my outrage. This is the beginning of our radical thinking and action. In the wake of Loretta's death, some of my friends decided to run a series on gender violence to open up the conversation and help move it along. Emotions were running high, and we felt compelled to act. Our first piece was Tara Williamson's "Don't Be Tricked." It was a brave piece of writing. It was raw, because we were raw. It was angry, because a lot of us were angry. I could personally identify with every word of Tara's piece, particularly the line "The system and most Canadians don't give a shit about you, how strong and talented you are, how hard you've worked, or where you live. If you are an indigenous woman, you are a prime target for colonial violence." This is something I've felt my whole life and never articulated.

I've never articulated it because I don't want young indigenous women and queer youths to know that; I want them to feel hopeful and empowered. I've never articulated this because I don't want white Canadians to automatically blame indigenous men for gender violence. I know they will because they've invested a lot of energy into the stereotype of "Indian men" as unfeeling, uncaring, violent savages. They've invested even more energy into pretending that they themselves don't benefit from colonial gender violence perpetuated by the state. In fact, they've invested a lot of energy into pretending that colonial gender violence perpetuated by the state isn't even a thing. I also don't want indigenous men to tell me I'm wrong or that this issue doesn't matter, because as much as this is a political issue, this is an intensely painful and personal issue for anyone who has survived gender violence, which if we are honest, is most of us, including indigenous men. I don't want to have to seek out allies in white feminists, who don't really get it. I want indigenous men to have my back, even when they feel uncomfortable about what I am saying. And you know what? A few of them did, and that was one of the most amazing feelings I have ever had. They emailed support. They checked in. They listened and encouraged. They retweeted, posted, wrote, and expressed their outrage.

This is co-resistance.

This is community.

White supremacy, rape culture, and the real and symbolic attack on gender, sexual identity, and agency are powerful tools of colonialism, settler colonialism, and capitalism, primarily because they work efficiently to remove indigenous peoples from our territories and prevent reclamation of those territories through mobilization. These forces have the intergenerational staying power to destroy generations of families, as they work to prevent us from intimately connecting to each other. They work to prevent mobilization because communities coping with epidemics of gender violence don't have the physical or emotional capital to organize. They destroy the base of our nations and political systems because they destroy our relationships to the land and each other by fostering epidemic levels of anxiety, hopelessness, apathy, distrust, and suicide. They work to destroy the fabric of indigenous nationhoods by attempting to destroy our relationality by making it difficult to form sustainable, strong relationships with each other.

This is why I think it's in all our best interests to take on gender violence as a core resurgence project, a core decolonization project, a core of any indigenous mobilization. And by gender violence, I don't just mean violence against women; I mean all gender violence.

This begins for me by looking at how gender is conceptualized and actualized within indigenous thought, because it is colonialism that has imposed an artificial gender binary on my nation. This imposed colonial gender binary sets out two clear genders—male and female—and it lays out two clear sets of rigidly defined roles based on colonial conceptions of femininity and masculinity.

This makes no sense from within Anishinaabeg thought, because first off, we've always had more than two genders in our nation and we've also always practiced fluidity around gender in general. The rigidity seen in colonial society doesn't make much sense within an Anishinaabeg reality, or the reality of any so-called hunting and gathering society.

Anishinaabeg women hunted, trapped, fished, held leadership positions, and engaged in warfare as well as engaged in domestic affairs and looked after children. They were encouraged to show a broad range of emotions, and express their gender and sexuality in a way that was true to their own being, as a matter of both principle and survival. Anishinaabeg men hunted, trapped, fished, held leadership positions, engaged in warfare, and also knew how to cook, sew, and look after children. They were encouraged to show a broad range of emotions, and express their gender and sexuality in a way that was true to their own being, as a matter of both principle and survival. This is true for other genders as well. The degree to which individuals engaged in each of these activities depended on their name, clan, extended family, skill, interest, and most important, individual self-determination or agency. Agency was valued, honored, and respected, because it produced a diversity of highly self-sufficient individuals, families, and communities. This diversity of highly self-sufficient and self-determining people ensured survival and resilience that enabled the community to withstand difficult circumstances.

Strong communities are born out of individuals being their best selves.

Colonialism recognized this and quickly co-opted indigenous individuals into colonial gender roles in order to replicate the heteropatriarchy of colonial society. This causes the power and agency of all genders to shrink, and those who are furthest away from colonial ideals suffer and continue to be targets of harsh colonial violence.

People also had agency over their sexual and relationship orientations in Anishinaabeg society, and this created diversity outside the heteronormative nuclear family. Anytime your hear or read an anthropologist talk about "polygamy" in indigenous cultures, read this as a red flag, because you need a severe form of patriarchy for that to play out in the way the anthropologists imagined, and in the absence of that, plural marriage or nonmonogamy in indigenous cultures is something far more complex.

There wasn't just agency for adults. Children had a lot of agency. When a chaplain came through my territory, he was appalled because the women and children were so far outside the control of the men that he interpreted this as a bewildered, chaotic, societal disaster; he interpreted us as "savage." I imagine him observing our society and asking from a white, European male perspective: How do you exploit women as a commodity in this situation, when they have such agency?

You can't.

Then I imagine the colonizers asking the next logical question: How do you infuse a society with the heteropatriarchy necessary in order to carry out your capitalist dreams when indigenous men aren't actively engaged in upholding a system designed to exploit women? Well, the introduction of gender violence is one answer. Destroying and then reconstructing sexuality and gender identity is another. Residential schools did an excellent job on both counts.

Because really what the colonizers have always been trying to figure out is: How do you extract natural resources from the land when the people's whose territory you're on believe that those plant, animal, and minerals have both spirit and therefore agency?

It's a similar answer. You use gender violence to remove indigenous peoples and their descendants from the land, you remove agency from the plant and animal worlds, and you reposition *aki* (the land) as "natural resources" for the use and betterment of white people.

This colonial strategy is clearly working. We also have more than eight hundred missing and murdered indigenous women in Canada, a mass incarceration of indigenous men, and we do not even have statistics about violence against indigenous two spirit, LGBTTQQIA, and gender-nonconforming people. I think it's not enough to just recognize that violence against women occurs but also that it is intrinsically tied to the creation and settlement of Canada. Gender violence is central to our ongoing dispossession, occupation, and erasure, and indigenous families and communities have always resisted this. We've always fought back and organized against this— our grandparents resisted gender violence; our youths are organizing and resisting gender violence because we have no other option.

Feminist scholar Andrea Smith recently wrote a blog post in response to Eve Ensler's One Billion Rising about what organizing against gender violence should look like.

Several of her points resonated with me.

Her post first encourages us to acknowledge that the state is the primary perpetrator of gendered violence in our nations and thus the state cannot be the solution to gendered violence. The state is not our ally. White feminism is not our ally either, because discussing violence against women without discussing gender violence within a colonial context has no meaning for me. Gender violence and murdered and missing indigenous women are a symptom of settler colonialism, white supremacy, and genocide. They are symptoms of the dispossession of indigenous peoples from our territories.

Some families of missing and murdered indigenous women want an inquiry. I respect this because Canada must be forced to be accountable for this crisis. Canada must change. Canadians must change their attitudes toward indigenous peoples and their relationship to us as nations. I also have little faith that the federal government has the capacity to undertake an inquiry that will bring about the kind of action and change indigenous peoples are demanding, and address the root causes of gender violence. The process in British Columbia has been a disaster, and we simply cannot allow an inquiry to be used by the state to neutralize indigenous dissent, mobilization, and protest. The perpetrators of colonial gender violence cannot be in charge of coming up with a strategy to end it because they are the beneficiaries of it. We therefore need a multipronged approach to our organizing. If there is an inquiry, we have to organize and mobilize through it.

And while it is important for us to come together to honor and remember our missing sisters and their families, I also feel angry about this situation and how violence, both symbolic and real, has impacted my own life. Rather than seeking recognition from Canada for this pain and suffering, I feel compelled to use this anger to build nations and communities where violence within our interpersonal relationships is unimaginable.

Communities where we see environmental destruction and contamination as a form of sexualized violence, because toxic chemicals and environmental destruction compromise the integrity of our territories and bodies.

Communities where we see dismantling settler colonialism as central to ending gender violence, because let's remember that gender violence is still a primary strategy used against us in our mobilizations, and you can find examples at Oka, at Elsipogtog, and in the Idle No More movement.

We cannot create movements, like Idle No More, where women are in leadership positions and where we also have no plan in place to deal with gender violence in an effective manner. Particularly when we know, from four centuries of experience, that gender violence will absolutely be part of the colonial response, and that this violence will not necessarily be perpetrated against women in leadership roles but rather against the most vulnerable women—those who are dealing with multiple sites of oppression.

This realization came crashing down on me during Idle No More when I got a phone call from another woman in the movement asking for help because an Anishinaabekwe had been abducted and sexually assaulted in Thunder Bay. The attack was racially motivated, and this woman was targeted in direct relationship to the activism around Idle No More.

It became really clear to me really quickly that not only do I personally lack the skills to deal with gender violence but that our community lacks these skills as well. The male leadership in the area was primarily concerned with calling for calm so that the situation didn't spark more violence.

I felt anger and mobilization was the correct response, but my first concern was with this woman and her family, so I called Jessica Danforth and asked for help. The Native Youth Sexual Health Network came through in practical, powerful, and beautiful ways, centering on support for the survivor and action on the part of the wider community. This story is in part included in *The Winter We Danced: Voices from the Past, the Present, and the Idle No More Movement*, along with all the resources that Native Youth Sexual Health Network provided us, and we're also donating the royalties from that book to this organization.

This is why youths are so critical to resurgence, because they are teachers and leaders in their own right, and because if we are carrying out resurgence properly, each generation should be getting stronger, more grounded, and less influenced by colonialism, and this means people like me can learn from them.

This is why resurgence is about bodies and land.

We must build criticality around gender violence in the architecture of our movements. We need to build communities that are committed to ending gender violence, and we need real-world skills, strategies, and plans in place, right now, to deal with the inevitable increase in gender violence that is going to be the colonial response to direct action and ongoing activism. We need trained people on the ground at our protests and the land reclamation camps. We need our own alternative systems in place to deal with sexual assault at the community level—systems that are based on our traditions, and do not involve state police and the state legal system.

Loretta Saunders wanted an end to gender violence and missing and murdered indigenous women. I am not murdered. I am not missing. And so I am going to honor her by continuing her work, and fighting for indigenous nations and a relationship with Canada that is no longer based on violence, heteropatriarchy, and silence. I want to help build indigenous communities where all genders stand up, speak out, and are committed to both believing and supporting survivors of violence and building our own indigenous, transformative systems of accountability.

We simply can no longer rely on or expect the state, the largest perpetrator of gender violence, to do this for us.

Loretta Saunders is our tipping point.

#ItEndsHere

Spread the

Miracle

Spread the Miracle: Abolish the Police

Anarchist Jews wrote this piece for a Chanukah ritual/action in solidarity with Ferguson and against police brutality, organized by Jewish Voice for Peace and others in Seattle on December 16, 2014, the first night of this eight-day festival of lights.

You will smash the roof of the villain's house,
Raze it from foundation to top. Selah.
You will crack the villain's skull with Your bludgeon:
Blown away shall be his warriors,
Whose delight is to crush me suddenly,
To devour a poor man in ambush.

—Habakkuk 3.13–3.14

Every twenty-eight hours, the police shoot a black man. The recent revolts against the murders of Michael Brown and Eric Garner have reignited the continual fight against racism, injustice, and the police. In Seattle, the police execution of John T. Williams, a native man, Oscar Perez-Girion, a Latino man, and others are burned into our collective memory.

"Mai Chanukah? What is Chanukah?"

Chanukah tells the story of the victory of a few warriors against an empire; the momentary triumph of light over darkness. Quickly, though, the victors—Hasmoneans (Maccabees)— reconstituted themselves as state power, reigning as kings, against those they had supposedly liberated. Chanukah is the possibility of a miracle—the triumph over enemies no matter how great. It is also a warning of what happens when a struggle does not recognize that all those who take power are its enemy, or in today's terms, that this is a struggle against the police, prisons, borders, and all those institutions that keep us in chains. So, Mai Chanukah? It is the possibility of the impossible, eight days of light when there could only be one, the possibility of true freedom in the face of the "all-powerful" state.

The Jewish history of expulsion, genocide, and ghettoization bears witness to the fleeting nature of rights and privileges. On this continent, the persecution of colonized peoples, native people, black people, and all others who do not fit into legality and rights as determined by the state will not be resolved through an appeal to the state for rights and privileges, because those in power can take and give as they see fit. The mere history of the police as slave patrols for black people shows the complicit nature of the system in white supremacy.

For non-POC Jews who would welcome an identification with whiteness: Has the lifting of quotas, end of ghettoization, and removal of structural anti-Judaism at the end of the 1960s in the United States really erased a history a couple thousand years in the making? There is a difference between acknowledging white privilege and identifying with the oppressive apparatus that is white supremacy. The importance of this "privileged" moment is not just to question our role but also to be openly opposed to whiteness by aligning with insurgent aspects against white supremacy—comrades of color, antifascist Jews, and rebellious white people.

"Eitz chaim hi, lemachazikim ba."

From Morocco in the Melahs to Lithuania in the shtetls to Poland in the ghettos, Jews have created autonomous and self-sufficient communities of mutual support. The Jewish values of the celebration of life, the quest for survival, and Tikkun Olam grant us the ability to pursue the light of justice, the foundation of all existence.

For the destruction of the police and the white supremacist system they protect!

Happy Chanukah! Black Lives Matter.

Rest in Power: Mike Brown, Eric Garner, Oscar Perez-Girion, Oscar Grant, John T. Williams, Tamir Rice, Aiyana Jones, and all victims of the police, borders, and states.

127

Spread the Miracle

In Support
of Baltimore

In Support of Baltimore; or, Smashing Police Cars Is Logical Political Strategy

This piece by **Benji Hart** was posted on April 26, 2015, on the Radical Faggot blog, radfag.wordpress.com, and after "going viral" and drawing lots of commentary, was followed by a related post, included below, on May 4, 2015.

As a nation, we fail to comprehend black political strategy in much the same way we fail to recognize the value of black life.

We see ghettos and crime and absent parents where we should see communities actively struggling against mental health crises and premeditated economic exploitation. And when we see police cars being smashed and corporate property being destroyed, we should see reasonable responses to generations of extreme state violence and logical decisions about what kind of actions yield the desired political results.

I'm overwhelmed by the pervasive slandering of protesters in Baltimore this weekend for not remaining peaceful. The bad-apple rhetoric would have us believe that most Baltimore protesters are demonstrating the right way—as is their constitutional right—and only a few are disrupting the peace, giving the movement a bad name.

This spin should be disregarded, first because of the virtual media blackout of any of the action happening on the ground, particularly over the weekend. Equally, it makes no sense to cite the Constitution (that document was not written about us, remember?) in any demonstration for black civil rights, but certainly not one organized specifically to call attention to the fact that the state breaks its own laws with regard to the oppressed on a nearly constant basis.

But there is an even bigger problem. Referring to Black Lives Matter protests as well as organic responses to police and state violence as "nonviolent" or "peaceful" erases the actual climate in which these movements are acting, militant strategies that have rendered them effective, and long history of riots and direct action on which they are built.

I do not advocate nonviolence—particularly in a moment like the one we currently face. In the spirit and words of militant black and brown feminist movements from around the globe, I believe it is crucial that we see nonviolence as a tactic, not a philosophy.

Nonviolence is a type of political performance designed to raise awareness and win over the sympathy of those with privilege. When those on the outside of struggle—the white, the wealthy, the straight, the able-bodied, the masculine—have demonstrated repeatedly that they do not care, are not invested, are not going to step in the line of fire to defend the oppressed, this is a futile political strategy. It not only fails to meet the needs of the community but also actually puts oppressed people in further danger of violence.

Militancy is about direct action that defends our communities from violence. It is about responses that meet the political goals of our communities in the moment and deal with the repercussions as they come. It is about saying no, firmly drawing and holding boundaries, demanding the return of stolen resources. And from queer liberation and black power to centuries-old movements for native sovereignty and anticolonialism, it is how virtually all our oppressed movements were sparked and has arguably gained us the only real political victories we've had under the rule of empire.

We need to clarify what we mean by terms like "violence" and "peaceful." Because, to be clear, violence is beating, harassing, tasing, assaulting, and shooting black, trans, immigrant, women, and queer people, and that is the reality many of us are dealing with daily. Telling someone to be peaceful and shaming their militancy not only lacks a nuanced and historical political understanding, it is literally a deadly and irresponsible demand.

The political goals of rioters in Baltimore are not unclear—just as they were not unclear when poor, black people rioted in Ferguson last fall. When the free market, real estate, elected government, and legal system have all shown you that they are not going to protect you—in fact, that they are the sources of the greatest violence you face—then political action becomes about stopping the machine that is trying to kill you, even if only for a moment, getting the boot off your neck, even if it only allows you a second of air. This is exactly what blocking off streets, disrupting white consumerism, and destroying state property are designed to do.

Black people know this, and have employed these tactics for a very, very long time. Calling them uncivilized and encouraging them to mind the Constitution is racist, and as an argument fails to ground itself not only in the violent political reality in which black people find themselves but also in our centuries-long tradition of resistance—one that has taught effective strategies for militancy and direct action to virtually every other current movement for justice.

And while I don't believe that every protester involved in attacking police cars and corporate storefronts had the same philosophy, did what they did for the same reasons, it cannot be discounted that when there is a larger national outcry in defense of plate glass windows and car doors than for black young people, a point is being made. When there is more concern for white sports fans in the vicinity of a riot than the black people facing off with police, there is mounting justification for the rage and pain of black communities in this country.

Acknowledging all this, I do think events this weekend in Baltimore raise important questions for future direct and militant action in all our movements. In addition to articulating our goals along with crafting our messaging and type of action, we need to think carefully about what the longer-term results of militant action might potentially be. Strategies I might suggest, and important questions I think we should try to answer as we plan or find ourselves involved in political actions, are these:

Are we harming state and private property, or are we harming people, communities, and natural resources? Is the result of our action disrupting state and corporate violence, or creating collateral damage that more oppressed people will have to deal with (that is, black families and business owners, cleaning staff, and so on)? Are we mimicking state violence by harming people and the environment, or are we harming state property in ways that can stop or slow violence? Are we demonizing systems or people?

Who is in the vicinity? Are we doing harm to people around us as we act? Is there a possibility of violence for those who are not the intended targets of our action? Are we forcing people to be involved in an action who may not want to be or are not ready?

Who is involved in the action? Are people involved in our action consensually or simply because they are in the vicinity? Have we created ways for people of all abilities who may not want to be present to leave? Are we being strategic about the location and placement of bodies? If there are violent repercussions for our actions, who will be facing them?

We should attempt to answer as many of these questions as possible before action occurs, in the planning stages if possible. We also need backup plans and options for changing our actions in the moment if any of the agreed-on conditions are not the same when it comes time to act.

I rolled my eyes when inquiries in Ferguson "shockingly" revealed racist emails sent throughout local government, including higher-ups in the police department. I think many of us knew the inquiry of virtually any police department would yield almost identical findings. The riots in Baltimore have many drawing parallels between policy and conduct in both cities now. What kind of action brought to light for the less affected what black people have always known? What kinds of actions will it take to make it widely understood that all policing is racist terror, and that justice can only come with its permanent abolition?

Black power, queer power, power to Baltimore, and to all oppressed people who know what time it is.

What the Movement Still Teaches, What the Movement Still Needs

Last week, my piece "In Support of Baltimore," addressing militancy and the uprisings in Baltimore, was shared more times in twenty-four hours than most things on my blog have been shared in years. It struck a chord I had not predicted and challenged the poisonous narratives that were dominating the airwaves last weekend.

Afterward, I got death threats. I got called a nigger, and a few conservative sites found my Facebook profile and reposted pictures of my image. Fox News called for an interview, as did the *Huffington Post* and several radio shows. I declined most of these offers, not only because I didn't trust the goals of the outlets, but also because centering my voice was not the point.

"A riot is the language of the unheard," many were surprised to learn Martin Luther King Jr. said famously about black riots in 1968, after being encouraged by media to calm protesters. Perhaps even more poignantly, James Baldwin stated in an interview with *Esquire* that same year, "If the American Negro … is going to become a free person in this country, the people of this country have to give up something. If they don't give it up, it will be taken from them."

Some objectors to my argument made cliché appeals: "both sides need to be held accountable" or "violence only begets more violence." Many revealed they had not actually read the piece, or at least not carefully.

Virulent responses to using the word "racist" to describe those criticizing the riots made it once again evident that "racist" is still seen as the worst insult one can call another in this country, when it shouldn't be. We are all products of a racist society, all say and do racist things regularly. The only way to actually end racism is learning to recognize it in all its forms, to name it in ourselves and others, not for the sake of shaming individuals, but instead to accept responsibility for our own roles in its perpetuation.

Let us once again be clear: if we oppose violence, then we must oppose all forms of policing. If we oppose violence, then we must call for an end to war, an end to occupation. We must oppose sexual assault, and prisons as institutions that wield it as a strategic tool. If we abhor violence to bodies, families, and

communities, then we should abhor all these systems and call
for their immediate abolition. As Ta-Nehisi Coates said so perfectly
in his *Atlantic* piece "Nonviolence as Compliance," "When
nonviolence is preached by the representatives of the state, while
the state doles out heaps of violence to its citizens, it reveals
itself to be a con."

Other writers challenged some of my views in important
ways—not by defaming rioters, but rather by acknowledging
that rioting is rarely something that can be planned or controlled.
Understanding riots, militant uprisings, as emotional reactions
to extreme trauma as much as political demonstrations was an
important point of reevaluation for myself—one I feel I am still
learning about from other writers, community members,
and activists.

My heart is heavy at the end of this week over the indictments
of six officers in Freddie Gray's case, not because I do not believe
in individual accountability, but because I, too, believe that
violence begets more violence. As a movement, we cannot celebrate
indictments for any crime. If we seek to end racist policing, we
must seek the end of all policing, all incarceration. We have got to
comprehend this once and for all. When we call out the violence
in some of the state's representatives while heralding others as
our heroes, we are falling for its tricks. We are reinvesting in
its authority, which means we are fortifying our own ultimate
subjugation. Instead of invoking the names of our dead to call
for more imprisonment, we need to tell their stories in service of
demilitarizing, decriminalizing, and freeing our communities
from the prison system forever.

Some—in most cases, conservatives and policing advocates
who had not actually read my article or fully grasped it—tried to

make the issue about me this week. It didn't work, because the issue is not about me, just as it is not about individual police officers, the state's attorney, or individual slain black people.

A movement cannot be about one voice. It is never lead by one leader. The moment we are in inspires me so deeply because there are innumerable leaders. At the forefront are women, queers, and young people of color. We are genius, we are loud, and we are tirelessly action oriented.

There are too many of us to imprison, too many of us to arrest. There are too many of us to censor, to smother with senseless sound bites, to demoralize with propaganda. There are too many of us to intimidate with the very violence that our movement seeks to eradicate.

Don't let them make you forget that.

Solidarity,
as Weapon
and Practice,

versus
Killer Cops
and
White
Supremacy

Solidarity, as Weapon and Practice, versus Killer Cops and White Supremacy

This piece by **Cindy Milstein** is a greatly revised version of a post on their Outside the Circle blog, cbmilstein.wordpress.com, written during the height of nightly street demos and freeway shutdowns in the Bay Area in solidarity with Ferguson.

On December 10, 2014, after a four-hour march from downtown Berkeley to downtown Oakland, the FTP ("fuck the police") demo was winding down. Then, suddenly, some protesters outed two undercover cops, one of whom got spooked. He whipped out his gun and aimed it at the demonstrators. His dramatic pose was captured in a journalist's photo, speedily shared on social media.

This incident is surprising and not surprising.

The cops seemed tired; they admitted it themselves in a December 9, 2014, news story. They'd been pushed to their limits by our large protests, which by that time had cost the Oakland Police Department $1.36 million extra in overtime.

The dynamic movement across the continent sparked by the Ferguson revolt is raising the social and economic costs of police assassinating black and brown people on a daily basis without any cause beyond white supremacy. Millions are stepping up their engagement—from walkouts at schools and shipyards, to blockades and property destruction targeting "the whole damn system," to new Copwatch and disarm-the-police initiatives.

It's also widely revealing the emotional and personal costs for people who've lost loved ones to murderous police. (As my scholar-activist friend Lilian Radovac notes, this includes a "funeral poverty" cost, since many of these same people are poor and can't afford whatever rituals of mourning feel best.) For them, these costs are nothing new. They've known long and intimately that "it's not one bad apple; it's the whole damn tree." Within the space pried open by a movement, their words and grief are now made exceedingly public. What's been painfully self-evident to them and their ancestors for the whole of colonial and US history has fueled vigils and riots, die-ins and uprisings. And it often puts rage and sorrow within inches of (killer) cops' faces, as many of these families and friends are front and center at demonstrations.

This movement isn't stopping; it's spreading.

It is not surprising, then, that according to media, exhausted cops are "freaking out" and making such "mistakes" as drawing guns on protesters. Nor is it surprising that uniformed cops are shooting "nonlethal" bullets at demonstrators—bullets that injure, and have been known to permanently maim and kill. For the moment, police forces are on the defensive. The only way for them to regain control is to bring their hidden violence (hidden, at least, from those who don't face it daily) into the light of protests.

That is why, unsurprisingly, the police are getting more serious about using every weapon in their toolbox, from ammo to lies, to crush this social movement.

Their violence is not surprising. Cops are increasingly using guns as "shoot-first" protocol, daily executing black and brown people—not to mention other nonwhite and indigenous peoples, queer and trans people, the poor and those in mental and/or physical health crises. This is why people are placing their bodies in the streets as a massive exclamation mark: "Enough is enough! It has to stop!"

Nor is it surprising that the police are none too happy in the spotlight we are shining on them. They are, in fact, enraged at a movement that's questioning their social control, their very existence, by asserting and occasionally experimenting with strong communities that make policing obsolete. The institution of policing itself is the precise target of this movement.

And they know it.

So when exhausted and cornered, they're going to get even more freaked out. They're going to be sloppier, which often makes them more violent. And they won't care, based on their correct belief—backed by courts, states, the nonprofit-industrial complex, and other top-down power brokers—that they are immune to criticism, much less responsibility, much less suffering consequences when they kill people.

The thing that *was* surprising that night when people faced down a cop brandishing his gun was the response of some of the protesters themselves. Too many of them didn't, and still don't, get it. Before the dust had even settled, they broke the ranks of solidarity and took the side of the police against a certain group of protesters.

As opposed to talking and tweeting about the courage that it took to confront plainclothes cops, these self-appointed authorities—"peace police" as they're known in radical circles—circulated myths about outside agitators. The undercover cops were there, they said, to instigate looting and other forms of "violence" that would discredit the supposedly law-abiding protesters. They ignored the actual facts: several protesters, at grave personal risk, had exposed undercover cops; the cops, in turn, had instantly exposed their inherent violence by pulling out a lethal weapon; those who revealed them were acting out of solidarity to protect their antipolice accomplices. Instead, the peace police used the incident to turn on protesters with whom they had political disagreements. They used the police as a weapon, whether unthinkingly, out of habituation, or to advance their own agenda.

How can this incident not firmly underscore the very reason we're already on the streets? How can the overwhelming, everyday evidence supplied by killer cops caught on YouTube videos and phone cameras not convince people that police systemically neither serve communities nor protect rights? How can anyone believe we are *provoking* cops with unpermitted marches, overturned dumpsters, or FTP banners when *they* initiate violence repeatedly, routinely? And how can such lived experiences not be binding us closer and deepening our distrust of cops?

But the "peaceful" protesters ally themselves with cops, apparently unable to see the relationship between the *institutional* patterns of cops as killers, cops as violent enforcers of everything from white supremacy and heteropatriarchy to capitalism and colonialism. Paradoxically, these demonstrators don't appear to see what likely most inspired them about Ferguson and Baltimore: the fierce *contestation of power*—a contestation that was not asking the brutal powers-that-be to try to act nicer but, conversely, was resolutely taking back occupied neighborhoods and struggling to dismantle the brutal system of policing within them.

So without question, the police dogging our protests are going to bare their teeth. That should be an unremarkable given, not even worth a chant of "shame, shame, shame."

They are also going to smile and use another, sharper weapon in their toolbox: divide and conquer. That, alas, is one of the best tools: getting us to police each other so we'll unravel our own movement for them.

This tried-and-true means of neutralizing social movements takes many forms. Its premier one, though, is leveraging our own socialization within a white supremacist, heteropatriarchal society—whatever our "identities"—against us. Police can nudge this along, explicitly and in the shadows. Or they can sit back and let all that we're taught *not* to see—the myriad of hegemonic assumptions deeply socialized into us from birth—coupled with generations of painful wounds, work their magic to disappear rebels and rebellions alike.

At a minimum, then, we need to continually remember why we are on the streets to begin with: cops kill, every single day in this United States, with near-complete absolution. They do it to uphold the current systems of social organization. Such structures have, from the start, stolen lands and stolen lives in the name of colonialism and slavery, social control and social domination, wealth and power for some, and misery and impoverishment for the many. Recalling this is crucial to all of us seeing more perceptively, through the lens of those written off as disposable by a relatively small gang of elites and their armies.

This may sound obvious. Yet as the #BlackLivesMatter hashtag has illuminated, there's much that everyone can't see. And so the healthy debates around, for one, whether #BlackLivesMatter refers only to black male lives, or also black female lives, or also black queer and trans people's lives, and so on. A thoroughgoing critique of police as institution would have both every life lost to cops and specific patterns of violence matter simultaneously. The beauty of a social movement is that it opens up reflexive space for us to undo ourselves, becoming the new people better capable of inhabiting the new society we're struggling to create.

If we are to make radical change (as in "relating to or growing from the root")—whether we're striving toward a future liberatory society or fighting to end murder by cops today—we'll need to frustrate the logic of the state and its police apparatus. We'll need to draw from other memories, whether cultures of resistance or examples of actually existing autonomous, caring communities. And we'll need our own divide-and-conquer strategies, with the vast majority of humanity on our side.

Our toolbox is far more humble. It's a makeshift kit, pieced together by lost-and-found wisdom and experimentation, and filled with seemingly haphazard, broken tools. As social movements have nonetheless proved, those fighting for their lives and land are ingenious; they're good at making do with little because they've been forced to. A little can become a lot. Stones and feathers and hands have stood strong against heavily armed invaders, whether in the Occupied Palestinian Territories, Mi'kmaq and Elsipogtog nations, or Saint Louis suburb occupied by the National Guard.

For us many, solidarity is an especially strong weapon. It is probably our best one.

Even if the state doesn't have a full monopoly on violence, as anarchists of old contended, it has a vast arsenal of violence, ranging from chemical weapons and tanks to torture and drones, from endless numbers of guns to endless numbers of prison cells and psychological warfare techniques. Such stones, feathers, and hands are impactful because they are backed by relational solidarities, where trust has been built over time. By wielding this weapon of ours—not merely in name, but unfailingly and substantively in egalitarian practice—we increase our odds of "survival pending revolution," as the Black Panthers called their social programs.

Solidarity is what initiated Ferguson protests across this continent and beyond; it's what is keeping our fires of resistance burning, fueling our dreams of a new world. Solidarity has built a movement against killer cops and white supremacy, and that's no small feat given the legacy of genocidal racism in the formation and maintenance of the United States. If we can craft smarter, stronger, more empathetic barricades of solidarity to sustain us, we might just succeed in walling out the world of hierarchical social forces intent on breaking us down and ripping us apart.

So how can our varied organizing efforts—strategies and tactics arising from manifold political perspectives and aspirations—better encompass a generous attitude toward each other? How can a full sense of solidarity, or a unity in our diversity, be practiced in the form of organizing itself—the process of getting from "here" to "there"? How can our organizing avoid blurring into a liberal universalism, remain focused on whose bodies are most affected systemically, and yet not reinscribe the very hierarchies we oppose through various identity politics, allyship, and patronage models, or ideological and organizational insularity?

In short, how do we practice a solidarity that's compassionate *and* revolutionary: walking side by side *and* tangibly undermining white supremacy with each step?

During the "distant" era of the global anticapitalist movement in the 1990s to early 2000s, people tried to bring Zapatismo into their understandings of how to work together— how to walk, while asking—in what became known as "horizontalism." Folks around the world, in directly democratic and confederated assemblies, eagerly hashed out the Peoples' Global Action Hallmarks, looking to allow for heterogeneous social movements and lifeways against the homogenization that "globalization" signaled. Various continental, regional, and city-based consultas, spokescouncils, and convergences picked up these hallmarks, which offered a humanistic frame without ignoring the disproportionate weight of social suffering.

One formation from that period, Montreal's Anticapitalist Convergence (CLAC), still actively exists today, despite political highs and lows, in part because it took seriously the connective solidarity of such hallmarks. Its "Basis of Unity," developed for mass mobilizations such as Quebec City in 2001, against the fortress-like Summit of the Americas, is not completely applicable to the Ferguson-inspired movement. The anticapitalist organizers— CLAC and its Quebec-based accomplice, the Welcoming Committee—had plenty of advance notice. Still, they choose to spend months before what they publicly called a Carnival against Capitalism helping to ensure that people with different organizing styles and tactical approaches could work together, and with grassroots neighborhood associations and Quebec City residents, toward a common goal: shutting down or disrupting the summit.

The solidarity afforded by the "Basis of Unity," hammered out and agreed to collectively in assemblies, is far more expansive then the present-day "protocols" written and released by small, self-appointed "leadership" groups of "white allies" and nonprofit-industrial complex nonwhite organizers. It holds out open arms of trust and promise, in contrast to the judgmental dos and don'ts of ally protocols. It is not self-congratulatory. It welcomes all, and encourages bold imagination and varied participation versus prescribing, for instance, what slogans or types of people are permitted at a direct action. And perhaps key, it makes transparent a radical social critique and social vision that serves as both organizing umbrella and leap of faith.

It directly asks, "Which side are you on?" and then lets you answer by walking, perhaps with missteps, but always shoulder to shoulder.

The "Basis of Unity" is committed to an inclusive, radical solidarity: "Respecting a diversity of tactics, the CLAC supports the use of a variety of creative initiatives, ranging from popular education to direct action and civil disobedience." The diversity clause, in essence, recognizes that an opposition to systemic domination, such as white supremacy and a police state, should take many forms if any sort of large-scale social revolution is to be forged. By embracing "education" and "action" equally—and thereby also breaking down the supposed theory/practice divide—the conflation of "militancy" with "radicalism" is shattered. One isn't a revolutionary because one is a militant. At any given moment, not all revolutionaries can take the same risks—but this is something that individuals must determine for themselves, without self-appointed leaders deciding in advance which "identities" can take what risks.

What this diversity of tactics translated into at that time was a diversity of people, not to mention growing an enormous and vibrant movement. It was not an assertion of difference for difference's sake—potentially implying a diverse movement emptied of content. The diversity of tactics notion instead supplied a guide to nurturing participation and unity in a way that was at once qualitative and sincere. It allowed the particular (then, the ways that free trade agreements hurt the human and nonhuman world; now, black lives matter) and universal (then, anticapitalism; now, abolishing white supremacy) to complement not crush each other—and struggle together for social transformation while concentrating squarely on whose lives do not matter, historically and presently.

This isn't mere wordplay. It was tangibly facilitated during the anticapitalist convergences of that day. To cite just one example, during the Quebec protests, there were three tiers of color-coded zones—yellow, green, and red—to indicate varying possibilities of arrest risk and militancy. That system was widely explained beforehand in assemblies, on flyers, and during the marches. All three "colors" were routed on the same street at first, walking together in a festive march. When the march got closer to the many-deep lines of riot cops guarding the world elites, the three tiers branched out, with "red" heading straight for the militarized fence. Many people who'd originally chosen a potentially "safer" contingent decided to stick with the red bloc, emboldened by the joy and strength of the numbers along the way, and even tossed teargas canisters back at the cops. And when the police failed to abide by the organizer-designated zones, red bloc folks came to the aid of those in "yellow" or "green" areas.

One could argue that the solidaristic ties cultivated in Quebec and elsewhere in Canada through the lived practices of the "Basis of Unity" allowed for later mobilizations to see and name more— for instance, to practice both anticapitalism and anticolonialism in a single action—and thus to agitate better. Solidarity can make hard and at times divisive conversations possible, or as indigenous anarchist Klee Benally observed at a talk I attended, allow for an "anti-retreat" from the conflicts that emerge in our spaces and organizing. And so, with "respect & tolerance for a diversity of tactics as a basic principle," according to Zig Zag of Warrior Publications, indigenous and nonindigenous people organized the No Olympics on Stolen Native Lands convergence in the Unceded Coast Salish Territories ("Vancouver") in 2010. The "stolen" staked out an antagonism to capitalist *and* colonialist theft. The convergence featured themed days with varying levels of potential risk, during which quite literally, indigenous and nonindigenous folks stood by each other in numerous planned and, movingly, spontaneous ways against the huge police presence. It made for the most qualitatively diverse week of actions in recent memory, such as the Take Back Our City march that saw an indigenous bloc flanked by both a black bloc and No One Is Illegal bloc.

Similar promises of solidarity have carried through to many other convergences around the world. It is worth quoting the "Pittsburgh Principles," drafted for the G-20 protests in 2009, in full for the breadth of its revolutionary solidarity and as a reminder of what's been lost today:

Our solidarity will be based on respect for a political diversity within the struggle for social justice. As individuals and groups, we may choose to engage in a diversity of tactics and plans of action, but are committed to treating each other with respect.

We realize that debates and honest criticisms are necessary for political clarification and growth in our movements. But we also realize that our detractors will work to divide by inflaming and magnifying our tactical, strategic, personal, and political disagreements. For the purposes of political clarity and mutual respect, we will speak to our own political motivations and tactical choices, and allow other groups and individuals to speak on their own behalf. We reject all forms of red-baiting, violence-baiting, and fear-mongering, and efforts to foster unnecessary divisions among our movements.

As we plan our actions and tactics, we will take care to maintain appropriate separations of time and space between divergent tactics. We will commit to respecting each other's organizing space, and the tone and tactics they wish to utilize in that space.

We oppose any state repression of dissent, including surveillance, infiltration, disruption, and violence. We agree not to assist law enforcement actions against activists and others. We oppose proposals designed to cage protests into highly restricted "free speech zones."

We will work to promote a sense of respect for our shared community, our neighbors, and particularly poor and working-class people in our community and their personal property.

This is not to claim that Pittsburgh and many other spaces of resistance have been able to fully follow through on their lofty principles. But they *aspire to try*, seeing such solidarity as part and parcel of any revolution worth fighting for, and as critical weapon in our arsenal to "serve and protect" each other as we strive to grow movements capable of fulfilling lofty aims, such as the abolition of police, prisons, and white supremacy, such as collective liberation.

Compare the "Pittsburgh Principles" from 2009 to how a well-known Bay Area activist chastised a 2014 "FTP Speakout & March against CHP" in Oakland. CHP stands for California Highway Patrol, which as it was soon discovered, was who the undercover cops outed on December 10 were. This FTP event was scheduled on December 13—the same day as the already-planned Millions March. The shared date made logical sense, given that it was a Saturday and thus more doable for many, and more important, given that both events agreed, "Oakland is Ferguson. Ferguson is Oakland," as the Millions March Oakland promo put it.

The FTP speak-out was respectfully scheduled to start about an hour or so *after* the stated end time of the Millions March. The speak-out portion was meant as a way to leisurely gather folks before the second march so as to give people a break to eat or rest if needed.

Solidarity, as Weapon and Practice

It also allowed time for those who didn't want to be in the vicinity of what might be a rowdier demo to steer clear, even though the Millions March was planned to end many blocks away. Both kicked off from Oscar Grant Plaza, renamed in his honor during Occupy Oakland, and now the go-to spot for most Oakland protests.

In spite of the sensitivity that went into this FTP action—quickly organized, it should be added, due to the rapid-fire developments—the seasoned activist told me that it was a clear case of not having respect for "a diversity of spaces." He added that the Millions March was going to be "peaceful" and the FTP one was going to be "smashy." (The Millions March turned out to be one of the more lackluster demos, even by "nonviolent" protest standards, and the FTP, thanks to a mobile sound system, became a huge and much-needed "reclaim the streets" celebration of our new movement's strength.) This activist also happens to have been one of the key organizers of the 1999 protests in Seattle, where civil disobedience in many concurrent forms, from lockdowns in the streets to shattering Starbucks' windows, disturbed the peace all right, but of the World Trade Organization meeting and police state defending it. The power of Seattle, like other pivotal moments, was that a diversity of humanity, with or without written principles, acted as if in revolutionary solidarity, smashing through the fine line that turns disparate protests into a global social movement.

Some of this activist's white ally friends chimed in: How dare the FTP, which they assumed (wrongly) was organized by whites, do anything at all on the same day as the "black leadership's" Millions March? As someone named Jon Jackson responded on the FTP's social media page, "[I] cannot believe people are getting upset over MORE demonstrations against police violence because

THEY didn't call them. Come on, folks."

The black leadership that initiated the Millions March—two black women in New York—was either far distant and/or hadn't especially been part of the nightly Ferguson solidarity protests, which isn't a criticism so much as a statement of fact. Those nightly, illegal marches of thousands—which went for many hours and miles—were responsible for catalyzing the movement here and hence creating space for a diversity of events. Images of the militant engagement in the Bay Area flew around the world—freeways brought to a halt, bonfires in the streets, and graffiti on walls. Black Oakland youths were a big part of the evening demos, and likely found it odd that the Millions March promised "a safe space for the Black Community," almost as if it hadn't been listening: there's no safe space for them in a white supremacist world.

Or as Oakland accomplice Ben Trovato remarked,

> Everyone wants to chant "Black Lives Matter," but it seems like no one really wants to follow the lead of black and brown youths in the streets—those kids who have the most likelihood of being the next Mike Brown or Eric Garner or Alex Nieto.
>
> How do we act in solidarity and confluence with what's already being played out in the streets? What would it mean to put aside our particular ideological and theoretical hang-ups, and just be out there, with and for these kids? How do we extend the logic and intelligence of what the movement has already developed, and really explore present dynamics rather than smugly judge?

Which is another way of saying that solidarity, to have any meaning in practice, demands active empathy as its foundation. As Leslie Jamison argues in *The Empathy Exams*,

Empathy isn't just remembering to say *That must really be hard*, it's figuring out how to bring difficulty into the light so it can be seen at all. Empathy isn't just listening, it's asking the questions whose answers need to be listened to. Empathy requires inquiry as much as imagination. Empathy requires knowing you know nothing. Empathy means acknowledging a horizon of context that extends perpetually beyond what you can see.

As predictably tedious as clockwork, after each uprising and riot, false dichotomies like "peaceful" and "smashy" protesters get tossed out by those who, whether they admit it to themselves or not, want to maintain the status quo with some progressive tweaks. The bottom line, for those who think and act from such binaries, is that it's not the tree; it's only the apples—the "bad" ones, whether they're in police forces or protest circles. There may be many reasons for this political stance—ultimately about only seeing and caring for oneself and one's own—but it is unquestionably antithetical to solidarity. Pointing out "our" bad apples not only does the work of state and police to destroy social movements; it quite literally *is* state and police work. As Shareef Ali of Oakland remarked back in late 2014,

> If you are at a protest and you choose to take pictures or record video of people doing illegal things, you may end up putting that person in jail. That is, because you disapproved of someone's behavior, because you thought it was "violent" toward inanimate objects, or because you thought it might hurt the movement, you are choosing to assist the state in sending that living, breathing person to one of the most violent places in the world, for the *express purpose* of destroying the movement. Even if you're right about the ethics or efficacy of

property destruction—and I don't think you are—that is totally, utterly unconscionable, and it is far more violent and counter to the cause of justice than smashing a window ever could be.

Empathy is the bulwark against this, for by taking the time to ask "questions whose answers need to be listened to," we begin to truly see why people protesting alongside us choose a particular tactic on a particular night in a particular place. We see a widening "horizon of context," complexity, and humanity. Empathy is "a choice we make: to pay attention, to extend ourselves," says Jamison. "[It] means we've committed ourselves to a set of behaviors greater than the sum of our individual inclinations [because] empathy means realizing no trauma has discrete edges. Trauma bleeds. Out of wounds and across boundaries. ... Empathy demands another kind of porousness in response." Solidarity.

A twenty-two-year-old black man, who'd grown up in what he calls the "hard" part of Oakland and had never left, decided to travel to Ferguson when the uprising started. On return, he marveled, "We got it good here. They've got almost nothing." Despite that, he explained, they look out for each other. To paraphrase one of his many stories:

Looting happened, sure. People feel abandoned. They were angry about Mike Brown's murder and lots more. But folks know which businesses are with the people and which aren't, even if outsiders don't get it. So they looted the businesses that exploit and overcharge them for things like food, because the owners know there's almost nowhere else to go and no way to get out of Ferguson. No public transit or anything.

Here's the thing: whole families looted together. All ages. People helped each other. They'd throw a blanket over a broken window to make sure people didn't cut themselves going in and out. They brought stuff to a central place and redistributed it according to need in their community.

One evening, at the peak of the Ferguson solidarity demos in the Bay Area, thousands marched to the Berkeley Police Department, chanting "Kayla Moore, Michael Brown, Shut It Down, Shut It Down." Kayla, a black, transgender woman with a history of mental illness, died—was likely murdered—in Berkeley police custody, so this stop at BPD was in remembrance and honor of her. There were many cops in riot gear blocking us from the building. It was one of those standoffs mainly about the catharsis of publicly expressing anger, which is after all part of the range of human emotions arising from loss and grief.

A young black man tossed a relatively harmless object at the police station and turned to run. A young white female stretched her arm above the crowd, pointing, and screamed loudly, "There he is. Get him! He threw something. Peaceful protest!" Hundreds of people and the cops started looking around for the guy to grab him. But two people put their bodies in front of the woman, blocking her view. "We're protesting against these police likely killing someone after an arrest, and you're turning a young black man over to them?" they asked her calmly. She stopped in her tracks: "I'm sorry. I wasn't thinking. I won't do that again." The young man got away.

At another night demo, a large army of militarized cops tried kettling some thousand marchers. The police had blocked off all four sides of a street, save for a small gap—a gap created by about a dozen anarchists, who had quickly placed themselves between the cops and protesters. As two demonstrators were scurrying out, one complained about how the anarchists were provoking the police and endangering the crowd. No, her friend corrected, they're making sure that no one gets arrested and also showing that people can stand up to police without fear.

Yet another evening, cold and miserably damp, a particularly small number of folks showed up for an antipolice bike ride through Oakland. The organizer circled everyone up first, asking if all had bike lights, because cops were ticketing-as-harassment, and if not, handing out loaners. Throughout the ride, he made sure we weren't getting separated and thus made vulnerable on our own. The bike demo went on for what seemed hours, constantly followed by far more riot police than cyclists. A helicopter, as always, followed overhead. Everyone felt dispirited. What the hell was the point? Just then the organizer circled us up again and enthusiastically noted, "We may not be shutting down the police station, freeways, or BART stations. We may not be many. But every night that we keep most of Oakland police out of neighborhoods where they assault and kill is a victory. It's what we should be doing all the time."

Solidarity, as our best weapon, is also a provocation that we can indeed begin to make police and white supremacy obsolete by experimenting in self-organization, whether in the many micro-moments we're handed by history, too frequently by police, to those grander approximations, such as when gangs called a truce in Baltimore against killer cops and for their neighbors. But it takes, to again cite Jamison, "exertion," "labor," "waking up in the middle of the night and packing our bags and leaving our worst selves for our better ones." Solidarity, as weapon, is a verb. It is also a form of love.

We are tired too, like those freaked-out cops, but not of the streets. We're not tired of fighting for what we know is just. We're weary beyond slogans of the violence of state, capital, and white supremacy. Solidarity should *not* look like us chanting "This is what democracy looks like," given that US-style democracy is murdering people at home and beyond, nor "Whose streets? Our streets!" given that the police state, colonialist and/or capitalist, has repeatedly stolen land. We need new models of self-governance and self-determination.

I want to walk in the streets nightly, exhausted and exhilarated, forging trust, becoming new people in a new culture that we're already prefiguring and holding strong against those forces that would destroy all that is life affirming.

I want to be part of what author James C. Scott calls an "anarchist calisthenics": staying in shape by breaking a "trivial law that makes no sense, even if it's only jaywalking, [because] one day you will be called upon to break a big law in the name of justice [so] you have to be ready." When we walk miles together in unpermitted marches with no police of our own, with no "states" or "prisons" in our head, we practice what it means to feel increasingly comfortable in breaking laws that aren't just, in defying a structural logic that is unjust by definition. In that way, we build up rebel muscles for the harder and harder fight ahead—the fight for freedom.

I want to love and rage, mourn and struggle, with millions of others, against this killing machine, until we shut it down for good—replacing it with social goodness that we can barely yet envision, and armed with do-it-ourselves, steel-hard solidarity as shield, aid, humanity, ethic.

Support AK Press!

AK Press is one of the world's largest and most productive anarchist publishing houses. We're entirely worker-run and democratically managed. We operate without a corporate structure—no boss, no managers, no bullshit. We publish close to twenty books every year, and distribute thousands of other titles published by other like-minded independent presses from around the globe.

The Friends of AK program is a way that you can directly contribute to the continued existence of AK Press, and ensure that we're able to keep publishing great books just like this one! Friends pay $25 a month directly into our publishing account ($30 for Canada, $35 for international), and receive a copy of every book AK Press publishes for the duration of their membership! Friends also receive a discount on anything they order from our Web site or buy at a table: 50% on AK titles, and 20% on everything else. We've also added a new Friends of AK ebook program: $15 a month gets you an electronic copy of every book we publish for the duration of your membership. Combine it with a print subscription, too!

There's great stuff in the works—so sign up now to become a Friend of AK Press, and let the presses roll!

Won't you be our friend?
Email friendsofak@akpress.org
for more info, or visit the
Friends of AK Press Web site:
www.akpress.org/friends.html